BUTCHER, P. 17 LOPES, P. 31 FITZGERALD, P. 45

BODY & SOUL

SINGER, P. 57 ANDERSON, P. 69 BANE, P. 79 VADEBONCOEUR, P. 89

BODY & SOUL

TEN AMERICAN WOMEN

ALVAREZ, P. 101 BELLE DE JOUR, P. 113 ROSS, P. 123

Text by
Carolyn Coman

Photographs by
Judy Dater

Design by
Lance Hidy

Hill & Company, Publishers • Boston

Credits

Edited by Toby R. Gordon
Proofread by Lee Carr
Lettering of main title by Sumner Stone
Production by Lance Hidy and Peter Carr
Printed by the Meriden-Stinehour Press
Bound by A. Horowitz & Son
Publicity by Alice Acheson

The Typeface: *Body & Soul* is the first book published in **Stone Serif**. This new typeface was designed by Sumner Stone in the PostScript language at Adobe Systems, Inc. The Stone typeface family consists of three groups: Serif, Sans, and Informal. Each is available in three weights for both the roman and italic.

This book was written, edited, designed and typeset using Macintosh computers, and Quark XPress for page makeup. First proofs were done on a LaserWriter Plus; reproduction proofs on a Linotronic 100.

Library of Congress CIP Data
Body & Soul
1.Women—United States—Interviews. 2. United States—Biography. 3. Women—United States—Pictorial works. 4. United States—Biography—Portraits.
I. Coman, Carolyn. II. Dater, Judy. III. Title: Body & Soul
CT3260.B63 1988 920.72'0973 87-32696
ISBN 0-940595-13-3 (cloth)
ISBN 0-940595-16-8 (paper)

Hill & Company, Publishers
121 Mt. Vernon Street
Boston MA 02108

Acknowledgments

Special thanks to Julia Siebel, whose generous support helped make *Body & Soul* possible.

We would also like to thank
Mark Alexander,
Laura Bauman,
Robert Blake,
Marc Blane,
Phil Block,
Carolyn Bonier,
Brother Benedict,
Debbie Collins,
Anna Coman-Hidy
Abigail DeWitt,
Barbara Ettinger
Vanessa Gamble,
Anne Gordon,
Ann Grace,
Sylvia Greene,
Basil Hedrick,
Diane Hidy,
Steven Holt,
International Center of Photography,
Diane Johnson,
Henry Korn,
Georgianna Lagoria,
Tom Luddy,
Wah Lui
Dan McConnell,
Susan Monsky,
Monty Montee,
Anne Nadler,
Stan Roach,
Sam Samore,
Gay Schoene,
Janet Shea,
Louis Silverstein,
Donna Stein,
Lad Tobin.

We dedicate
Body & Soul
to all our
women friends,
and to our
teachers,
Arno and
Imogen.

Introduction

By Carolyn Coman

"There is *nothing* you can possibly say that the priest has not heard before," the nun reassured my second-grade class. We were just about to make our first confessions. I swallowed her promise with equal measures of relief and disbelief. I loved feeling that we were enough alike to have words, thoughts, and deeds in common—especially ones that might require forgiveness. All the same, I knew we were not *that* alike: we each had more or less nerve, different versions of "who started it," limits to our show and tell. I counted on everyone having her own story. I still do.

Isn't diversity, after all, a

giant relief, a gift that in the giving makes room enough for us all? I count on the differences that make other lives seem inspiring and wondrous, outrageous and heartbreaking. I count, as well—perhaps even more—on the connections that enable us to understand other lives.

"Sometimes you think, Is this life real? Or is this just a play?" Vickie Singer asked this question in wonderment as she told her story, a story that pushed against the borders of any imagined version of real life. She spoke in acknowledgment of the fact that sometimes forms blur; you forget just what ball park you are in, and one game resembles another—fiction, nonfiction, real life, art. *Body & Soul* was conceived and made with such blurring in mind, in form as well as content. We wanted a form that would satisfy with words and pictures together, drawing on elements of cinema, documentary, biography, oral history. We wanted a nonfiction work with the appeal and embrace of fiction.

Body & Soul began as a collection of interviews and portraits of women in nontraditional jobs. Judy and I worked with a dozen women before we admitted to each that we wanted *more:* whole lives, and not necessarily lives defined by nontraditional jobs. We were drawn to women who were thoughtful about why they were the way they were, and to life stories that couldn't isolate work without dragging in everything else—family, sexuality, politics—along the way.

Even after shedding our original premise, we struggled with the notion that we needed one unifying theme for our book: *Survivors* or *What Women Want.* Ultimately, we stopped our search for a single, electric thread because we did not want to stitch up our women's lives with it. We became more interested in running a gamut than in toeing the line—any line. And so we never settled on a convenient handle with which to yank up the book and carry it around. We settled, instead, on finding different things from different lives, contrast *and* connection.

First we imagined the kinds of women we wanted to meet—a

woman who breaks all the rules and doesn't give a damn, a woman who has, above all, endured, a champion. Together we drew up a list that included a broad range of experience, background, and philosophy. We were not after one of everyone, ten representatives who would somehow give collective voice to the female experience. We were looking for thoughtful perspectives on interesting lives. Our choices, constrained only by time, budget, and space, were ultimately personal.

With general categories in mind, we started talking to people—at work, at parties, at a funeral—asking for recommendations and gathering leads. We became accustomed to the excited interruption, "Oh, you should talk to..." or, "I heard about a woman once..." If the description sparked us, made us want to know more, we'd start to track the woman down. We were usually only two or three people away from her—a few phone calls, a letter or two. *You* know the woman we want to meet—she sits next to you on the bus, she is your mother, she is you. We operated on the assumption that there are rich stories all around us, and were not disappointed. We went on instinct, gut feeling about whom to include. If we had a screening process, it was, Do we want to know more? Can we sit in this woman's kitchen and talk the way women do? Can we make an unbelievable-sounding life understandable? Can we dig inside a quiet story and find adventure?

Ordinary, daily life ultimately made the sensational story understandable and human. And it was the drama within the seemingly ordinary life that inevitably floored us. We followed up a lead for one reason and invariably discovered other, unsuspected, sometimes deeper veins to follow as well. The stories we made in pictures and words were not usually the ones we thought we were going to get. And the divergences real lives made from our initial, general categories mattered not at all. We opted, over and over again, to let each woman be, rather than make her fit our preconceptions. There were times I wanted to reach out, catch a woman's words, and put them back in her mouth—words that offended my own viewpoint, or goofed up my growing understanding of who that woman was, or echoed a stereotype I did not want to confront. But we learned that to make the book we said we were after, we had to let people say what they said and look how they looked. We ended up with lives that went beyond our expectations, for better or worse, the way it goes in real life too, because real life is so much more complicated than stereotypes.

For many of the women in *Body & Soul*, it was the offer of fair representation—their lives, in their own voices, on their own terms—that inclined them to participate. I wrote the monologues using each woman's own words and shaped them according to whom I saw that woman to be. I was interested in subjective "takes" on a life, not in objective fact checking. The final stories, rendered from one form (interview/conversation) into another (monologue), are agreed-upon versions that satisfied both teller and listener—each of them approved by each of the women. Some did not change one word of the story I wrote, some made minor changes to clarify. Several made cuts to protect people other than themselves. But all revealed a great deal of their lives, making public much that is often kept private.

In the course of interviewing, transcribing, and finding a woman's individual story line, I always experienced a time of falling: into her voice, attitude, vision. Whether I agreed or disagreed with her became unimportant. What mattered was finding the sense of her story and telling it honestly. In working toward understanding, I grew to love every woman I came to know. I still hear Vickie Singer's voice, fast, pinched, adamant, "Oh, the pressures of being different"; "Mo" Anderson's Oklahoma drawl, slow and liquidy, "Learning to work was the name of the game"; Doreen Lopes' compassionate whisper, "I'm saying this as gentle as I can say it"; Gloria Vadeboncoeur's poetry, so heartbreakingly succinct, "I hope someday to be happy."

Listening to every voice, I visit again every place we traveled to in making this book: Alaska, Utah, Oklahoma, New Mexico, California, New York City. I remember every motel room of dead air, preachers on the television, my first taste of moose meat in Alaska. At a bar in Oklahoma I was struck by the beauty of the men as they danced the two-step—how much they communicated with so little movement. They echoed what I was learning: how much we give ourselves away, with every word, gesture, expression, in what we do as well as what we hold back. I was humbled, again and again in making *Body & Soul*, by all that people carry within them.

The women in this book do not know or have anything to do with one another. But they have all, in the end, offered themselves up for us to look at and listen to, bounce ourselves off of, maybe run from or run toward. And each of us is in cahoots with each of them as we enter their lives and form our impressions, as we find what is common and what is not. We think about them, feel about them, because of who *we* are, what our values are, where and how we were raised. Consciously or unconsciously, we compare our lives to theirs, use them to determine our own outlines, to show us ourselves in relief. When we like or dislike certain women, approve or disapprove of others, we give ourselves away every bit as much as they did.

I count myself privileged to have been with these women; and I count more than ever on the power of careful listening and looking to make sense of lives—others as well as my own. Working on *Body & Soul* led me to feel that connections are bigger than differences. Differences are obvious. Quickly apparent, they nudge, disturb, amuse. What is common bubbles up more slowly, often commanding less attention than different voices and various pasts. But basic connections—loving, working, surviving—make travel into the territory of wild difference possible. In the midst of all our extravagant variety, ordinary encompasses extraordinary, and compassion encompasses all.

Photographer's Preface

By Judy Dater

As a child, I always loved picture books and comics. I was a slow reader and felt impatient having to wade through a lot of words to get to the point of a story. I wanted the pictures to tell it all, yet leave room for my own imagination to fill in the details. As I gradually came to appreciate the special magic words carried, the kinds of images they alone could invoke, I often wished for books in which words and pictures carried equal weight. I found this fusion in film, but not in books—and this dynamic fusion is what we were after in *Body & Soul*.

To achieve this, Lance and I worked on the book's design even before Carolyn and I began interviewing and photographing the women. We discussed the variety of the pictures we would need and how we would integrate the photographs with the text. Having this kind of information ahead of time played a crucial part in the kinds of photographs I made.

I never believed that a single photographic image of a person could capture and define that person. A portrait to me suggested only limited things about the sitter; it was a poetic, fictionalized fusion of what the sitter projected and what the photographer wished and hoped to portray.

Most of the portrait work I had done before *Body & Soul* represented my personal choices of subject, based primarily on how the individuals looked. I was a kind of casting director, picking people to represent certain types—the possessive mother, the powerful yet vulnerable businessman, the macho laborer. I cast my subjects in roles that seemed natural to them but were not necessarily "who they really were." Their image became a representation of type.

The women Carolyn and I chose for *Body & Soul* did not always conform to my personal sense of what a "type" should look like—yet here they were, the real thing! Neither did they all, at first, inspire me visually. At times I despaired of ever making good photographs of them. But the demands of *Body & Soul* enabled me to see people through the camera in a new way, expanding my notion of what a portrait, or a series of portraits, could capture. Working with each woman over a period of several days rather than several hours gave me an opportunity to tap into her personality in a way never before possible. The incredible range of human feeling and experience showed on their faces like the markings on a seismograph. Where previously I felt I wasn't able to photograph certain people successfully, I came to feel I could photograph anyone if I could spend enough time with her—if I listened to her, if I understood her.

The premise of *Body & Soul* is to give equal voice to a wide range of beliefs. The differences we encountered were vast:

politics, life-styles, religions, attitudes toward sexism and racism. I wondered if I could be equally neutral and sympathetic to every woman. Could I suspend judgment, become impartial, and treat each woman with identical respect and fairness?

At times I strongly disagreed with views these women held; at other times I found them to be informative, entertaining, enlightening. Ultimately my deepest desire was to show each woman in the fullest spectrum of possibility that she allowed us to see. Above all I appreciated and valued the trust these ten women had in us, to make their lives visible and public, to give us permission to measure and examine our own lives and choices against, or in harmony with, theirs.

Photograph of Judy Dater on page 12 by Meridel Rubenstein, © 1988

BODY&SOUL

Susan Butcher

One night, in the fall—it was about nine o'clock and twenty below, pitch dark and blowing—I took a dog team on a trail about seven miles up into the mountains. It had started snowing, and the wind was blowing so bad I couldn't see anything. I thought I had better go home, so I looked for a place wide and flat enough to turn around.

It was early fall training, so the dogs were pulling me on a four-wheeled cart instead of a sled. (As soon as the snow is deep enough, I switch to a sled for the rest of the training season.) I gave the team a "haw" to turn into the hill, hoping we had enough room to turn. I thought I would let the four-wheeler roll backwards, whip around, and then jump on it, but we just went right over a twenty-foot cliff! I dragged the last bunch of dogs down. The dogs were OK. I was a little hurt, but nothing major.

There was no way to get the four-wheeler out. It weighs 550 pounds. The bottom of the cliff was all trees, and I had no survival equipment. I didn't have a knife, I didn't have anything. I knew I had to keep working—it was way too cold to stay there. I couldn't leave the dogs. The top dogs were barking and yanking to go. The bottom dogs were hanging halfway on the road, halfway on the cliff. I untied them all and got them up on top, lengthened out the gang line, just monkeyed around with the equipment that I had. They knew that we were in a bad predicament; they sense what's going on. I realized that David, my husband, didn't know where I was, and there was no way he could follow my tracks—I couldn't even see my tracks from where I had been five minutes before.

I found the little repair kit that they give you with a four-wheeler—pliers and a screwdriver—and I chopped down nine small trees with a screwdriver! My headlight was going on batteries, so I had to do it all with about the power of a match. Every once in a while I would flick it on to see what I was doing and then flick it off. The screwdriver was one of those ones where the pointy part is not attached to the handle. So every three hits the front part would fly out into the snow, and then I would have to feel around for it. I was getting really cold then. It was the most ridiculous thing. But I figured that if I got those trees down there was a chance the dogs could pull me out. They'd move me an inch, and then I'd hit a tree, and then I'd get through it. It took ages, but they just worked with me and got me out. It was about two in the morning when I got home.

By this time David was out looking for me. He knew I was in trouble. You never think about a person being dead. You think about them being in trouble. We discussed it later, and he said it would have been a week before he would have looked for me on that trail. I always carry a saw and an ax with me now.

When I came to Alaska twelve years ago I knew I wanted to run the Iditarod Trail Sled Dog Race. The Iditarod is a race, over 1,100 miles from Anchorage to Nome, that I had read about in a dog-mushing journal. I didn't know anything else about Alaska except that you could mush dogs up there, and it sounded much better than Colorado, where I'd been living. So I packed my bags and flew into Fairbanks. It was more of what I was looking for than I ever knew existed. Alaska is a place where you are your own person. It doesn't matter who you are related to or who you know. Your base of acceptance is your own ability to excel.

I'm not aware anymore of how different my life is from other people's until I go somewhere else. So many people don't seem to like their life. They are caught in something, and when they look at their options, they are just looking at options that are in a really tight little circle. They aren't looking at big options. And then they look at me and they say, "I'd love to do something like what you do." A lot of people think my life sounds great. It isn't that they want to be a dog musher, it's that they are lacking control over their lives. I think that you should try doing what it is that you want to do—so that when you're sixty you're not sitting back saying, "I should have been doing something different." That's all—so if you died tomorrow you weren't holding something back.

There are people up here who like me for who I am. There were lots of people who loved me back East, but we didn't have a real home base when I was growing up in Cambridge, Massachusetts. My parents got divorced when I was eleven and my sister was thirteen. My sister left home when she was fifteen, and I eventually left because I was looking for something else. I found it in Alaska, and with David.

I had the contrast of growing up in Cambridge in winters and Maine in summers. I disliked city life. In the country I was happy. I loved the people in the country, too. My grandmother in Maine had a tremendous influence on me. All during my life I have gotten along with individuals, but not people as a group. With people came fences, rules. My earliest memories are of wanting to live in the country and spend time with my dog, or any animals. During my parents' divorce, my first dog grew to be my mainstay.

My mother always says she doesn't know how she bore me. She is a psychiatric social worker. She thinks I am courageous because I go out into the wilderness. That's the last thing she would want to do, but we are really much alike. She did pioneering work in her own field. My

father is a hard worker and a gambler, like I am. He has incredible drive and competitiveness. I am the same way.

When I came to Fairbanks I worked at a musk-ox farm and started trying to get a dog team together. I wanted to go live out in the bush. I didn't know what the bush was, then, but I knew that it sounded great. I flew out to the bush with my four dogs, a friend of mine, a sack of flour, a slab of bacon, a few musical instruments, and that was about all. The cabin was fifty miles from the nearest road, close to the Canadian border in the Wrangell Mountains, and our closest neighbor—although we didn't even know it—was thirty miles away.

It was neat, getting to know a person that way. We didn't see another person for six months. We didn't see a jet fly over, a small plane, nothing. There was every type of wild animal every corner you turned. I have never been in anyplace that beautiful. I was lucky to have had that. Not many people will ever get to have it that good—if people think that's good. I did. For the first time in my life I had found it—utopia.

We didn't have a chain saw; we had to cut all our wood by hand. We knew where our food was coming from, and it wasn't a grocery shelf. Basically we hunted for all our food. The first winter I skinned the animals and helped haul them in, and by the second winter I was

killing at least half of the food, too.

We'd take saunas at forty below, chop a hole in the lake, tie ropes around each other, and jump in. We taught ourselves to play banjo and guitar. It was just life at its best. But even the first winter I knew that it couldn't last because I am too competitive and too driven. That life is great for a couple of years, to teach you where it all comes from. But once I knew, I needed to go further with it. I didn't want to ever leave the Wrangells, but I knew if I was going to race the Iditarod, things would have to change.

For part of the second winter I stayed there alone for a while, about a month. It was another experience that had to come along in life because I was still under the belief that I could live without people. When I was alone I was definitely lonely, but not unhappy, and definitely not lonely for any one person. I wasn't scared. I just had to be so cautious about not hurting myself, falling through the creeks and stuff. There were lots of wolves coming into my camp all the time, sometimes just ten or fifteen feet away, running parallel with me on the trail, and I was a little uncomfortable with that.

I always trust my dogs, especially my leaders. I have injured myself pretty good out on the trail, and I just call Tekla and the team back and let them lick my tears and my blood and see that I am injured. I tell them to line up, and I crawl into the sled, and they walk home, real slow and easy.

In Alaska people are tested. We are in danger a lot of times. We deal constantly with young death. Plane wrecks are real common, drowning is number one. Two of our dog-mushing friends drowned, not knowing they were on ice and breaking through. I almost drowned three years ago when I went through the ice and the river was sucking me under. You get scared, but you just try to figure out how to get out.

In November, while I was living alone, I mushed over to a friend's cabin about forty miles away to share a ptarmigan for Thanksgiving. I had never been on a forty-mile trip, and it meant I had to mush all my twelve dogs at once to get there, which I'd never done. It was a wonderful trip. It was over a mountain pass to get to my friend's cabin. I got into some bad overflow and got soaked up to my waist. I was way up above the tree line so there was no way to dry myself off. At dusk I found a shelter cabin, just slats, that slightly broke the wind. There was no wood to burn, so I took off all my wet clothes and brought the sled and all the dogs inside with me. I put four dogs in the sleeping bag with me—what the bush people call a four-dog night—to keep me warm and help me dry out some of the clothes I'd kept on. It was about twenty-five below.

In the morning when I got up everything I'd taken off was frozen solid. I had to tear part of the cabin apart and burn that and thaw things out. I couldn't dry my clothes, but I thawed them so I could get back into them. Then I finished the trip. There was no brake to the sled, and from the top of the ridge down was just a really hairy ride. It was great.

By the end of that second winter, as far as I was concerned I could take off anywhere I wanted in Alaska. I had learned anything that I thought I needed to know. I was ready to run the Iditarod.

I ran my first Iditarod race in 1978. I was twenty-two. I finished in the money in nineteenth place. Since then, I've always been in the top ten, with two second-place finishes. But it took me nine years to win. Many people hint that I should have won earlier, that I had the dogs and the ability. But I have always had my own rules. My father used to say, "You'll never win the Iditarod because you love your dogs too much and you are too honest of a person." But I believed that through breeding, training, and nutrition, I could win the race with my team being less tired and healthier than any team who finished behind me. I also wanted to win it with dogs I raised myself, and I felt I could still be friendly towards my competitors. In 1986 I won the race in my style. I reached my goal, setting a new world record of eleven days, fifteen hours, six minutes. My time was seventeen hours faster than the old record.

I have a very strong competitive side, and racing is a good way to use that up. To say that you want to win a race is a fine thing. It isn't showing hate or dislike towards anyone, it's just showing competitive spirit. I very much have that and I am at ease with it. I find if I am competitive a few times a year now—three or four races—I am relaxed and content the rest of the year.

For the last eight years I have lived in Eureka, 140 miles northwest of Fairbanks. I live in a small log cabin. I have no running water, and I heat with wood. Right now I have 180 dogs, 90 of which are pups. That's a lot of dogs, but I don't own a dog over the number that we can adequately take care of. Each dog gets a lot of personal attention, not just fed and watered. We let them loose all the time, and we run them in the teams almost every day.

Until recently I never had electricity, never had any mechanical conveniences. David has brought us the ability to generate our own electricity. These few modern conveniences give me more time to spend with the dogs.

People think I have this exciting, thrilling, glorious life. What appears

Susan Butcher's cabin in Eureka, Alaska

glorious to everyone else is so unglorious behind the scenes—feeding dogs, cleaning up after them. Our life is day-to-day, like everybody else's, and it is the day-to-day life I love.

I'm usually on the back of the sled all day. I'll take anywhere from two to six teams out and usually gross fifty to seventy miles daily. That's basically my life, and that's what I like. It's a good life here. I have built this place to be what it is, and I like it. The majority of the time, I can still be alone or alone with the people I choose to have around me.

David and I met in 1979, shortly after I came down from Mount McKinley. I had just taken a dog team to the summit. For years we were just real good friends. Somewhere along the line we fell in love. We have always had a great friendship and a good business relationship. I think that's a good, solid base for a marriage. There is a real romantic end to it also. So in 1985 we got married. So it's nice, and now I have that one person and that's all I need. Friends were always surmising as to what a man would have to be like to live with me. What I found in David is somebody with enough self-confidence to accept me as I am.

Being a top racer forces me to do a lot of things that aren't exactly my life-style. Money isn't something I want for itself, but it costs me a lot to run this kennel. I won prize money last year—but you can't count on that no matter how good you are. I sell dogs and that is another source of income. I also have to depend on sponsorship. I've been offered money by cigarette and booze companies. I've said no cigarettes, no hard liquor, so at least I haven't gone totally against what I believe in!

I dislike a lot of the media stuff. So much is just hype. I didn't choose to be famous. Just because I've been on

0
20
40
60
80
-20
100
-40
120
-60
°C
°F

"Johnny Carson," everybody has to ask, "What's Johnny Carson like?" I don't care! Why don't they ask me about dogs, why I like dog mushing, something I believe in? I don't even believe in Johnny Carson!

The media tries to make an issue out of the fact that I am a woman. The press almost always get my views of feminism wrong. For years, before David was in the picture, they always felt it was their obligation to know about my sexual life. There were hundreds of single men running the Iditarod, and they didn't feel they had any right to ask them. People ask such different questions to women.

I have a hard time saying I am a feminist, but why does anybody have to ask me? Why isn't my life just example enough as to what I believe in? I use the indirect approach and feel that I have gotten good results. But it has been a real struggle; I have fought hard for everything I've gotten, and I'm proud of what I have done. Yes, I am a woman, and yes it is a victory for me to win the Iditarod, but it *isn't* amazing—I did it because I am capable, and women are capable.

There may be plenty of men trying to stand in my way—and there have been—but I don't mind the pressure; it's an added challenge. It is each individual woman's battle at this point. Equal is the stupidest word that ever entered the male-female thing. I don't think it's a matter of equal; I think it's a matter of difference.

I am a real here-and-now person. I think about whatever is in front of me, and that's usually dogs. That's what makes me a good musher. I'm telling you about myself now because you're asking, but basically I'm not very introspective. I don't have a lot of time to think about things besides the moment-to-moment basic needs, and I think that is the best thing that ever happened to me.

Many people distort things way out of proportion by thinking and dwelling on them. One of the things that attracted me to country-living people were all the demands on them. The wood had to be hauled, and they didn't have time to dwell on all the other stuff. I think having to get on with work is beneficial in working through other things. That consistency in life makes you know that you are going to make it through everything.

I feel real good about where our life is now because I feel that we can just go in any direction we want. Do I really want to continue running the Iditarod? My belief is that I have it in me. If I had to state a goal in my life it would be to be the best musher.

David and I are interested in mushing in Antarctica. I am thirty-one and we want to have kids, maybe in the next five years. I want to do it right so the kids have the right sense of confidence and security and individualism—those are the most important aspects to me.

There are unhappy times in my life, but I like all the bad times, too. Those are the growing times. I don't know exactly what you learn, but you end up being who you are, and as long as you like who you are, how can you dislike what made you that? I learned total self-confidence. I am happy with myself. I know my faults, and I know my good points. I had to rely completely on myself, and I did it and I did it well. I know I was lucky, but I didn't see any holds barred, and I just went for it. I have total faith I can make it through anything that comes along.

Susan won the Iditarod in 1987, beating her own world record by thirteen hours.

Doreen Lopes

It was like living with a nightmare, like you killed somebody. The fear is always there. When I first told someone, I tried for about two hours to get it out. There was this terrible buildup, my heart was pounding. The woman thought I had actually killed someone. That's how hard it was. I felt ashamed. I was the only one who had the problem; it was my fault. Who but yourself that you knew?

Telling my kids was one of the toughest things. I break down just remembering it. My kids—I have three daughters—were young at the time. I couldn't read them a story. Couldn't register them in kindergartens or activities. I told them, "Mommy has a problem. She can't read or write or spell." They just said, "Mommy, it's OK, we'll help you." Then I knew I had to do something.

Now I am going towards my associate's degree. I'm halfway there. I know that getting that piece of paper will be the biggest day in my life. Be still my heart! I don't know if I will be able to get up there on that stage!

I wanted to give up a lot of times. My tutor told me I have to tell my professors that because of my dyslexia it takes me ten times longer and is ten times harder than someone with just the ordinary problems of going to college. It's true, ten times. But there is a fight in me, a drive, that I know I can do it. Right now I want that piece of paper so bad; I feel I deserve it. I may never use it in life, but I want that degree. Just to say I have it I guess.

I want to continue working in preschool, like I have been for the past fifteen years. I love working with little kids. They are so innocent. They don't have problems with race, they don't even think about color unless they have brought it from home. If I had had a teacher like me, I would have loved school. My kids love coming to school. I make it fun for them because it wasn't fun for me. I give them their first start, their foundation, and I give it my all. I'm a damn good teacher. But I really want to start working more with adults, in adult literacy, too. That's another goal I am working on. A lot of times I don't realize how far I have come. But I have so far to go, so much I should do.

Sometimes when I sit down and think about it, the bitterness comes out. Where would I be, what would I be doing, if I hadn't had to deal with illiteracy? That hurts a lot. I limit myself because I am afraid that I can't do something. I try but it is hard. Not reading stopped me from associating with certain people because I was afraid I wouldn't talk right, wouldn't understand them. Not reading stopped everything.

I grew up right here in Cambridge, Massachusetts. It was tough growing up, tough going to school with friends who knew how to read and spell, and I had to bluff my way. I was raised by my grandparents, who were from the old country, Cape Verde Islands. My parents divorced when I was very young. My grandparents could not speak or read English. I could write their names and my name, so they thought I was doing OK in school. At that time, I didn't know any better either.

When I was in third grade the teachers said they had to put me downstairs in the special class because I was undernourished. I was skinny. They never said anything about my education or reading or that I was slow. They just didn't know what to do with me. They put everybody together—the retarded, kids with seizures, behavior problems—they didn't care what age you were, nothing.

I hate that word, special class. Everyone called it the dumb class. So I knew that's what I was supposed to be. What else could you be but stupid? That's what they labeled you. Dumb. Stupid. Didn't want to learn. It drove me crazy. I don't know how I survived, to be honest with you.

The school that first put me in a special class is right near where I live now. They've made condos out of it. By rights, I should have one for nothing! That's how I look at it.

I was in the special class up to the seventh grade. Then they moved me to another school, supposedly seventh to eighth grade level. From there they put me in a girls' vocational school for two years. You were supposed to cook and sew and get married. They would have us read a paragraph or two now and then. I would know when it was going to be my turn and I would ask one of the girls, "What's this word?" and I would get it down before they called on me. Then I wouldn't have to feel embarrassed or ashamed. I got a diploma from there when I was sixteen. I kept the diploma because it was all that I had at the time and I thought it was OK. I realized later that it was not OK. I didn't know how to read or spell. I held onto it for a while, and one day when I started thinking about things, I tore it up.

I guess that God takes away and then He gives you something in return. I have a lot of strength, a lot of knowledge, even without the education that was due me. And I say due me because the Commonwealth of Massachusetts guarantees education up until the twelfth grade, and they didn't do it for me and many people like myself—they didn't do it for us. Here we have Harvard, MIT, Lesley, all these colleges—people come here from all over the world, and we can't even teach our own people? Kids come out of high school now and cannot read. That's pretty bad, pretty pretty bad. When I was sent to the girls' vocational school, they were sending people up to the moon, spending all this money on building

bombs. And they couldn't teach people like me to read? They didn't even know I couldn't read. Never tested me.

My dyslexia was never diagnosed until I found out that my daughter had dyslexia. When my daughter was having problems at school, I went to talk to the teacher about why she was being promoted from the third grade when she didn't even know how to read at a third grade level. I just went as a concerned parent, but I was labeled a troublemaker, which was fine. It's nice to be an honest troublemaker because you get things done. I would have told the world about my own problems to help my daughter. I didn't want her to go through what I went through. I walked out of her school with no results. It was February, snowing, and I cried all the way home. A girl friend of mine said there was something we could do. We went to the superintendent of schools. She came with me. I was nervous but I did all the talking; I told my whole story. My daughter was tested two days later.

To make a long story short, they found she had dyslexia—not a severe case of it, thank God. Dyslexia isn't just reading backwards. It's so many things—speech, hearing, coordination, fine motor skills. Well, it's also hereditary. Naturally, I thought, that's my problem. But I didn't get tested until a couple of years later. I was scared to death.

I did two days of testing at Mass. General Hospital, and I felt really bad, really low. I didn't do good. I was diagnosed as having severe dyslexia. I'm not supposed to learn as much as I have, not supposed to succeed so much. I had an argument with the doctor when he said I couldn't learn so much. I asked, "If I get up to a seventh grade reading level, can I go on? 'Well, the statistics say you can't.' Really? Well, if I can learn seventh grade reading, then you can't tell me I can't go on to college." I was always a fighter.

The first time I went back to Mass. General for tutoring, the woman who was supposed to tutor me did not show up. Didn't call me, nothing. The second time, she was there and she started right in with the tutoring. I said,"Excuse me, we can't do anything until I get this off my chest. I want to explain something to you. I'm here because I can't read. I don't know how to spell. But by no means am I stupid." I told her she should have had the respect to call me. After that there was no problem, we were great together. In my talks to students I make it clear to them: don't let anybody, anybody, make you feel ashamed of yourself; don't let anybody talk down to you. It's hard, because people do.

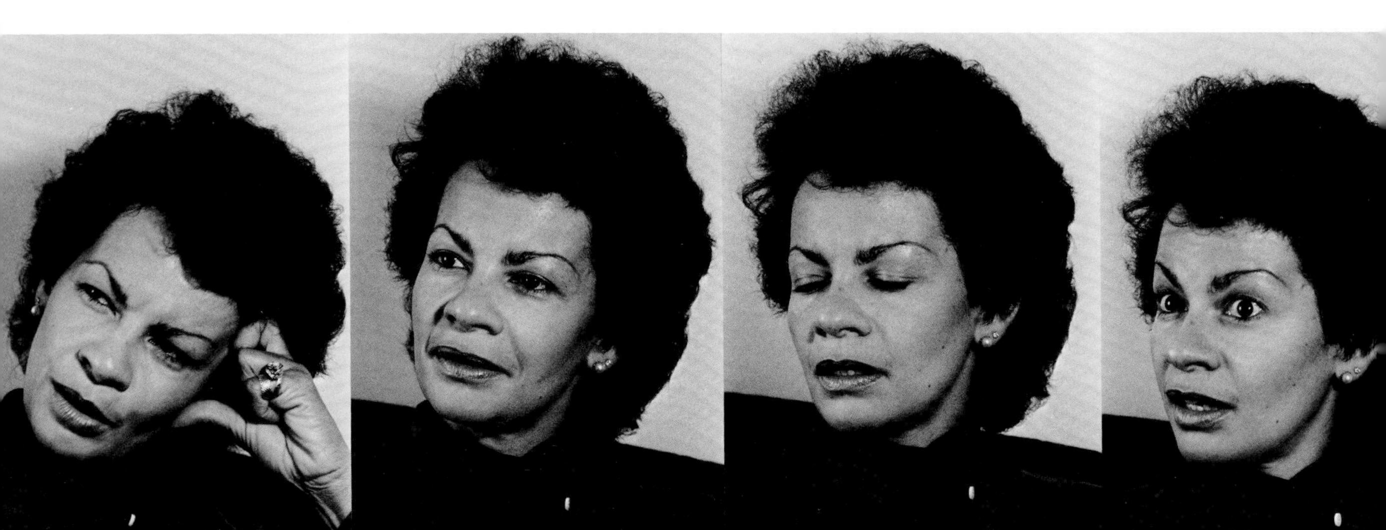

To show you how some people are very mean—when I was working at Headstart, I confided in the head teacher and told her my situation. Afterwards, the woman didn't like me and she did something I will never ever forget. I happened to look her way one day and see her talking to this kid who was asking her to write his name on the board. She coaxed him to come and ask me, knowing damn well I couldn't. I felt so bad. The feeling, I can't explain it. I held it for a long time. She was the head teacher and was jealous because parents liked me. Now that I am a head teacher, I don't do that.

There are people who don't stick up for themselves because they are afraid. That's what I am here for. I am here to help those people who cannot fight for themselves, cannot say to another person how they feel. I know how they feel, therefore I talk. If I see someone in a predicament and they can't fight for themselves, I'm gonna be right there, fighting for them. Especially in this situation.

I never used to talk. You talk about someone shy—yours truly. Shy shy shy. At one time in my life I stuttered so bad I could not talk. I would listen, but I wouldn't say much. But I still knew what was right and wrong and how to defend myself. I don't know how I overcame the stuttering. I didn't go to any specialist or any special class. I just did it.

But I knew what it was like for others. There was a girl in one of my classes who was retarded and she had—her face wasn't really nice, wrinkly skin, disfigured. No one liked her. I felt sorry for her, so I made her my friend. I knew that I was popular, kids liked me and stuff. I let them know if they wanted to be my friend they would have to be her friend. I know what it is to be hurt, even though my problem doesn't show.

I have more strength now that I am open about the problem because I don't feel ashamed like I used to, when I thought I couldn't learn. When I started getting help, I realized that it wasn't my fault—it was the system. To relate my story to others who have the problem, I have to be open. When I talk to groups about illiteracy and dyslexia, I tell them right at the beginning, here I am, but let me tell you, this took years, years for me to get here. And I'm still not where I should be.

Telling my story on a TV show about adult illiteracy was the best thing I did in my life—in terms of how I felt about myself and how I helped other people. Since I did that TV show, I feel like the whole world knows about me—no hiding, no lying, no closet anymore. And the station got feedback on it, lots of phone

Doreen at the preschool where she works in Cambridge, Massachusetts

calls. I personally helped ten people that I know of go back to school and maybe more people I don't know about. If I do nothing else in life, I did that. I'm proud of that.

The more I talk about it, the better it feels, but that hurt will always be there. There are plenty of nights I think about what I could have done, what I could do. I know I would have been doing something really powerful. I might have been in Washington. That hurts like hell—to know that you are intelligent and that you just weren't up-to-date in a society where education is everything. They had me programmed to believe that I was stupid. I knew I wasn't, but there I was in school and there was nothing being done. They didn't have special programs. I can't excuse the system just because they didn't know. It does not excuse them for letting people go through life the way I have gone through life. We are talking about millions of people, whether they have dyslexia or are just illiterate.

I used to act so well. Everybody acts, but I had to really act to hide this. Nobody knew. My own brother and sister didn't know. I hid it for years. "I don't have patience to read this," or, "My writing is so awful, oh come along with me and fill out the applications at my daughter's school, you know how I have trouble with forms." I should have been an actress. The only reason I wasn't is that I could not have read the script! There were years I would take any bus marked H and just hope it would be a Harvard bus. Now I can laugh, but it took me years to get here, years.

Hiding it was the work of my life. I was an expert. I bluffed my way through school, asked people, planned out my paragraphs in advance. Every place I went, you had to read this, write this. The fear was with me all the time. What a time I had, what a time I had. I don't realize it until I talk about it. It hurt. Hurt. You can't imagine.

People take it for granted that they can read. There is a lot of stuff I wish I had that other people take for granted. I always told my daughters to enjoy school, get everything out of it, because I never experienced a prom, don't have a yearbook. If I had gone to the regular high school, I know I would have been a cheerleader and all that. I hear a lot of people going back to their reunions. I don't have that to look forward to. To

me, if you can read, there's nothing you can't conquer in this world. I really believe that, I truly do.

I talk to both students and tutors about dyslexia and adult literacy. For a lot of the learning disability specialists, book learning is all they know. They haven't lived it. People with the problem—they know that I know how they feel. Deep down. I help them to bring up their bitterness. Some people don't even know they have it, but they do. You have to show your anger, have it come out.

When I was growing up, I didn't show my anger. It just stayed inside me. I was angry because my grandmother was old and sickly and I used to have to stay in the house a lot and clean. I couldn't invite kids in the house to play. I said when I had kids they would have a young mother and they could go out and play and I would do all the work—which wasn't true because my kids did their share. But my grandmother was very good to us. I didn't know it at the time. There is not a day that goes by that I don't think about her. She instilled values in me that I still use with my own children and other kids: respect, caring for people.

I didn't always get treated with respect when I was growing up. For a long time, I was bitter about the rape situation. I was five when it happened. I know there are things that happen to other people that are worse than my situation, but when you are going through things, the only thing you can see is your own situation. I did have a hard time. And I survived it.

My mother and father will be very surprised if they see this, that I remember the rape. We never discussed it, it's a closed issue. My sister and I are just starting to discuss it. For a long time we never talked about it either. We didn't know each other knew.

I remember I was playing on the stairs. This man comes down, he had his penis out, he was swearing, jerking himself off—I didn't know that at the time—and he made me put my mouth on it. And then all I remember after that is that I hated it. Holding me down, seeing that white stuff, I didn't know what it was. My sister said he did get into us, but I don't remember that part. Anyway, we got a disease, and we were quarantined. Everyone who came in the room had to wear a mask and a white uniform. All my sister and I remember was that we had oatmeal and we used to dump it in a bag to get rid of it. Kids will be kids.

I remember going to court; it's like it happened yesterday. I was so small, and the stand the judge was on was so high. I can remember him saying, "Little girl, it's OK, you can tell me." I told him. I remember the judge slammed the gavel down, and he said, "Get this man out of my courtroom and lock him up and throw away the keys." My sister doesn't seem to think the guy got sent to prison, but I remember the judge saying, "Throw away the keys."

After the rape, that's when the state took us away from our mother. I don't throw it in her face because my mother has paid for her mistakes, she has suffered. I don't blame her. When my brothers and sister get on her case about how she wasn't fit, she wasn't a nice mother, I get on them real hard. I have just as much right to be angry. But I am a mother and a woman and I realize that things that happen when your children are small, they're not always your fault. My father was no angel, either. My mother did not abuse us. She just wasn't ready to be a mother, is what I am saying. This is as gentle as I can say it without hurting my mother's feelings, if she reads this book.

There were five of us kids by my father. Later my mother had another set of kids. I am the third oldest. When the state took us away from our mother, they had to split us up. My grandmother took the three oldest—myself, my brother, my sister—and she raised us. And my other two brothers—oh I feel so bad about this—they had to go to the state. I can remember going to visit them. They weren't treated very nice, and here we were with my grandparents, and we were treated nice. We didn't have a lot of things, but we had love there. And then my two brothers didn't have it. They used to tie them up and beat them. I feel so guilty about that. I have for years. Even at a young age, it hurt so much. There were happy times, but there were a lot of sad times. Stuff I just can't forget.

There was another rape situation nobody knows about, not even my sister. I was thirteen. I used to pretend I was asleep, and this son of a friend of my aunt's used to come in and say, "It's the teddy bear," and he used to do things to me. I used to feel so...dirty. I see him now, and I am cordial to him. We greet, we hug. To this day he doesn't know that I know what went on, but I do. I know.

If any man were to touch my daughter, I would kill him. Outright. I would do it. Wouldn't think about it; I would have to kill him. And I am not a violent person.

There is just no way, no way that it would happen without something being done. No way.

I never had any therapy or counseling to deal with the rapes. I dealt with that myself. I don't know how but I did. I do a lot of crying. A lot of crying. Crying is good for you. I think I enjoy crying sometimes.

I'm willing to share some of these experiences because I think women need to know. We're all in there together. We're all human beings. I treat people like I want to be treated. That's how I get over things.

I should be bitter, but I'm not. I love people. I should hate men now. I should hate them, but I don't. I love 'em. I love 'em! What can I say? I will definitely get married a third time if the right man comes along. I'll try it one more time. I'm not putting all my eggs in one basket though. I've been hurt a lot of times. My sister-in-law used to tell me I fall in and out of love every other week.

My first marriage was a disaster. I was eighteen. My dream was to be a professional dancer. I did modern, jazz, toe, tap, ballet. I was good. I was dancing with a group the year my first husband asked me to marry him. He asked me to choose between him and my dancing. My group was going to Europe that year. I stopped dancing cold when I didn't go on that tour. They went to Europe and I didn't, and I have regretted that up to now. Again, it goes back to education. I didn't have that knowledge, that gumption to say, "I want to do that first." But then I guess it was fear, too—because if I went to another country, what would I do, how would I read things, get around? There were a lot of opportunities I didn't take advantage of because the fear was there. All through my life, you have to realize that the bottom was not knowing how to read or spell. The fear was with me all the time, even when I was having fun dancing and stuff.

Anyway, we got married. He was the one who abused me for not shelling his eggs in the morning. I was very stubborn, too. I know it takes two, but he had no right to hit me. That's how I got into doing volunteer work for battered women, because that was a cause I believed in. I wished they had it at the time I was going through my situation, but they didn't.

I left him when I was five months pregnant with our third child. I raised my children myself and lived in the projects. I cannot talk bad about projects because I had a good experience there, mainly because my kids didn't get into any trouble. I never believed in coffee cliques, people in your house. I had a lot of friends, but I didn't believe in having

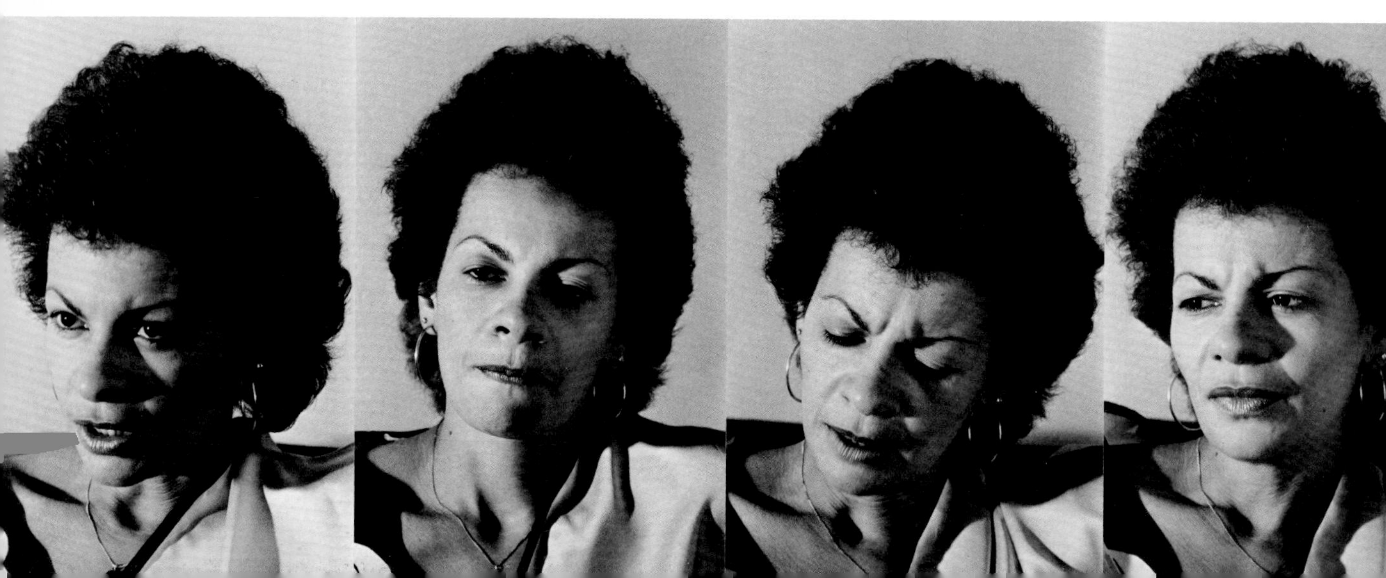

people come in and start talking, that's how trouble starts. I never borrowed. I was very independent. I had friends and family.

I was on AFDC. I had to start all over again. It was tough. As young as my daughters were, we really were close. They worked, they had to. It wasn't as bad as my childhood—they played and had company. When I was on my own with my children, I decided I had to do something with education. I was scared as hell, didn't know how to go about it. A social worker got me to my first tutor, Mrs. Peters. That's when I went back to school, no stopping. No one was going to stop me. I had been going to the Cambridge Adult Learning Center off and on for six years but never got that far because I always had some crisis in my life with the kids.

When I got married the second time, he said not to worry about going to school, he would always take care of me. Yeah! Need I say more? He was just a user—a person who uses other people. I thought I had met Mr. Right and come to find out he was leading a double life. I didn't know how serious it was. I used to drop him off to see the other woman. That hurt me more than anything—if you are going to do your stuff, fine, but don't do it in front of me, don't let me know. He just used me through the whole thing. I threw him out of the house.

I got my high school diploma that year—right before we split up. That was supposed to be one of the happiest times in my life, but it wasn't. One day I just said I may as well continue—I don't have any more babies, I am by myself, why not put that energy into learning, getting what I want, a degree. I just hope I don't pass out when I go on stage to get my associate's degree. I have to say that this last year and a half I have been very tired of being strong.

I still cry at night sometimes—even though I have come a long way. It has always been hard, and it will be hard. I cry at night because of what I could have been. I still don't give myself enough credit. I am very hard on myself. I guess I always will be, always thinking I should be doing more. I look at my resumé and I look at all the things I have done without reading and spelling skills, but still I am down on myself. If I had the education behind me, along with what I know about myself—because I like myself now—I'd be one hell of a woman! I am proud of myself at times, and people acknowledge me, and then I realize I am not that bad at all, I'm dynamite. But it goes in one ear and out the other. I figure if I give myself credit as much as other people give me, then I am gonna stop. I can't stop. I want so much.

Geraldine Fitzgerald

I remember sitting in a tree when I was about four. I had been getting a hard time from all the other children in our gang—I was a rather small and bullied child—and I didn't see much prospect of things improving in the near future. But while I was hiding in this tree, I thought, There must be other places than this place I am in. I could go to another place so I don't have to have the others knock me around. It was the first notion of, there is an alternate. I date the beginning of my life from that moment.

Since then I have constantly gone to other places. And perhaps that's what acting is—going to another place, finding and taking the psychological journey of another person.

I always wanted to act and direct. My father—a lawyer whose law firm appears in James Joyce's *Ulysses*—didn't terribly like the idea of my acting. My mother did. We were a Protestant and Catholic family, mixed, influences coming from everywhere. My mother's sister was a well-known Abbey Theater actress. My great-grandmother wrote serial novels—one, considered very dashing in the mid-1880s, about a girl who rode a bicycle! In Ireland people tend to be very individualistic.

I was educated in a convent in London that had many of the earmarks of prison. The nuns never wanted you to be alone. You were on your honor, but just in case your honor wasn't in good working order, they had spies. I remember writing to my mother and telling her some of these things and my amazement when the nun tore the letter up and said, "I am afraid that would make your mother

unhappy. Write another one." I became manic with the idea of getting out. Finally I got permission from my family to leave and attend the School of Art in Dublin. Looking back I can see that my parents were really very advanced.

In my youth I got sick a lot—typhoid fever, scarlet fever—until I was about fifteen, when the mother of a great friend said, "You get sick because you are afraid that you are going to fail." What she said hit like lightning. From then on, I determined to keep my appointments no matter what, sick or well, scared or not. And though my health didn't change immediately, I became able to say to myself, Even if I don't do well, I must never stop trying to do what I want with my life. If something is standing in the way of my getting what I want, I have to overcome it somehow—even if the "it" is me!

The theater that was around me in Ireland then was in full bloom—the theater of Sean O'Casey and all those wonderful actors, Barry Fitzgerald, F. J. McCormack, and writers, W. B. Yeats, Synge, and James Stephens. They were friends of my aunt. But instead of wanting to know them I wanted to go to the movies because I thought that the movie actors were really living those glamorous lives I saw on the screen, and I wanted to join them. The poetic tragedies of Yeats and the stark lives of O'Casey's slum characters in the Civil War were the realities around me in Dublin. I had no patience with the theater until I got to be sixteen or seventeen, when I fell in love with it. Then I knew that it was an art, that it was an illusion, and I was glad of it. I didn't want to be a movie star; I wanted a little dressing room with nothing in it but a shelf and some makeup and a chance to play in the works of the great dramatists I had once despised.

The parents of my best friends were the Irish equivalent of Virginia Woolf and her group—clever, intellectual, witty, and total perfectionists, all of them. They believed that unless one's talent was

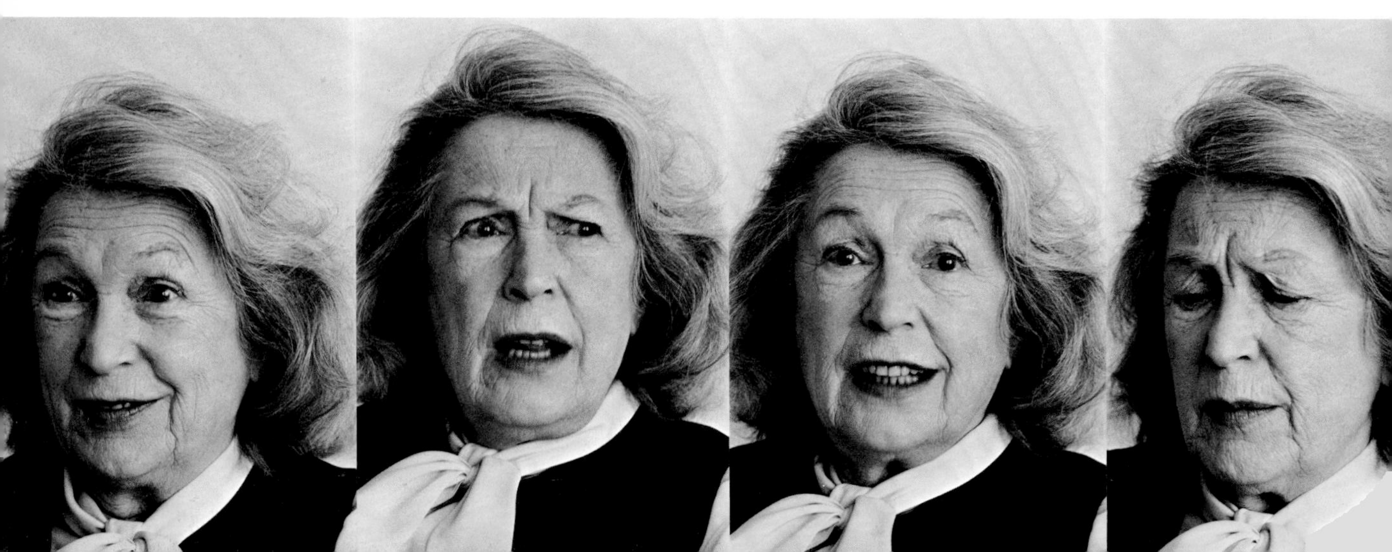

superabundant one should not even begin to try. I felt I should forget about my ambitions. So when my uncle, the playwright Denis Johnston, asked me how I was getting on with my acting, I told him I thought maybe I should give it up as I wouldn't really be good enough. He said, "That's a lot of rubbish. Do things in life because you want to, and even if the results are mediocre, you'll have much more fun doing that than spending your life contemplating other people's perfections."

From that time on, ironically, though I wanted to be in the theater, the movies kept intervening in my life. I couldn't get work in the English theater but I could in British films. When I came to America and joined Orson Welles in the Mercury Theater Company, one of the most creative theater companies of this century, with Vincent Price, Agnes Moorehead, Orson himself, John Houseman, and so on, I thought I had come home. But a theater like that needs governmental or civic support (which the Abbey Theater in Ireland and the National in England and Joe Papp's Public Theater in New York City have always had); and without that support we were all forced to go to Hollywood! It sounds funny because it is the dream of so many people to go to Hollywood; but our group didn't really want to. It worked out variously for us. Orson himself began to love it, came to like it better than any art form. I didn't like it at all. It wasn't theater.

I didn't have a hard time in Hollywood, I gave *myself* a hard time. I fought the people who tried to help me. Just like the parents of my childhood friends, I wanted every script to be perfect, which is hopeless, because no one can really tell a good movie from a bad one in script form—it is so much a visual medium. For instance (and I have to throw names around to tell you this story), when I was at Warner Brothers, I had lunch one day with Humphrey Bogart and Ingrid

Bergman. They were in despair, they could hardly eat. They were trying to get out of a film. She said it was absurd and ridiculous; he said it was rubbish. All I could say was, "Try, I hope you can." That was *Casablanca.*

I was offered magnificent things to do, and I turned down everything. I only took the role of Isabella in *Wuthering Heights* because the company said they would sue me for breach of contract if I didn't. That's the kind of dumb young woman I was! All I would say is, "I want to go back to the theater." Of course I regret not having explored all the opportunities I was given, but I don't think about it too often because it's no use. You absolutely can't change the past.

During the Second World War, I couldn't get back to Ireland, my husband was in Europe, and I had a little boy to bring up. By that time most people in the movie business in Hollywood were fed up with me, and I couldn't get really interesting parts. But I had to take whatever was offered in order to support my son. That went on until my contract expired. I left Hollywood then, and in 1946 I remarried and settled in New York.

I realize now I didn't always act wisely on my own behalf. I *thought* I was going after what I wanted, but as I looked at it objectively as I got older, I began to see that I acted in ways that would make it impossible to reach my goal. It's odd that one can build with one hand and destroy with the other and not be aware of it. It's not the way to live, always saying no. Now I guard against my self-destructiveness by saying more or less yes to everything. At least I have a much better time that way.

After I remarried and my daughter was born, I more or less retired from the whole business to bring her up myself. I felt I had not been as useful to my son as I should have been. During the war, I was the only breadwinner and could not spend as much time with him as I

wished. Later he would tell me of unhappiness in his childhood that I had not known of before. I thought it would be better if I more or less stayed at home, and so I did until she was old enough not to need me.

I wasn't afraid to retire, didn't fear that I would never be able to return to my own work. By that time I had learned that if you don't mind starting at the bottom of this mythical ladder we are all dealing with, then you can *always* begin again. It's not true that there is a lot of room at the top—there is very little—but there is *tons* at the bottom; and once you've found that out, you're never afraid. Oh, you may be a bit hurt with people not treating you so nicely. You may say to yourself, Do I have to go through all that again? But if you work at it long enough, you'll have a career again. Perhaps not in the favored position you once had—but you can get back.

Part of becoming any kind of an artist is an ability—that sometimes comes early in life—to step back from one's self. By that I mean something different from self-analysis. I mean trying to get back to the point of view of a very very young person, the person we once were before we tried to make ourselves over. Then one was in touch with one's unconscious. It has been said that geniuses are people who have greatest access to their unconscious.

In acting, you have your body and your psyche and that's it. You have no visible material outside of yourself. Consequently it is a very difficult art, an eternal, unending struggle to get it right. In fact, we can never "get it right," except, perhaps, a couple of times in our whole lifetime. But we remember those times and how thrilling it was. When it goes well with writing, you could almost take it up off the page and chew it, couldn't you? It seems to have its own shape and substance. While with painting and sculpture one's identity is absolutely transferred. But in the theater, the performance is always subjective, and we do not ourselves know when we are at our best or why. It's true that on the screen one can see one's image, but it has been edited by others and consequently is no longer one's own. In our profession, the realization is usually very far away from the concept. Maybe as far as we're

concerned we will never get the two to meet, but we keep on trying.

In our work, there is what we do and there is how it's perceived. But one's life is about what one does and not about how it's perceived. It doesn't matter what the critics say. If we do not feel our work is correct, we cannot be consoled by their praise. And if they don't like us, it creates a certain self-conscious anxiety which is not conducive to good work. So? So a great many actors seldom read their reviews. Of course it's lovely, fun, when others like one's work. And being known in one's profession adds a very pleasant dimension to one's life—strangers talk to you, you feel you have a lot of friends.

You don't know about success as a mother, either. My children have done extremely well—but as Bernard Shaw says, children mainly do that in spite of their parents. Whatever the reason, I know they are both doing what they both most wanted to do (one is a clinical psychologist and one is a director), and so I am very happy for them.

I know I've always loved my children, I know I've always tried, but I also know I have made bad mistakes. Perhaps it's unavoidable because one's own childhood is there to get in the way—just as it does with one's work and everything else, I suppose. In the play *Long Day's Journey into Night*, the mother, Mary Tyrone—a role I am in love with—says something that always strikes me as true. She says, speaking about her son Jamie, whose life has been a failure, "I suppose that life has made him like that and he can't help it. None of us can help the things that life has done to us, because they are done before you realize it, and once they are done, they make you do other things, until at last everything comes between you and what you would like to be, and you have lost your true self forever." For me, that's what *Long Day's Journey* is about, and that's what does happen to us all, if we are not fortunate enough to acquire some awareness.

I think some artists are somewhat aware of themselves and that gives them a bit of a chance. People who have the good fortune to be with a psychoanalyst have a chance. A good psychoanalyst is like a great detective who will help track down many of the causes of our failures and stop us from repeating our mistakes.

Geraldine Fitzgerald's living room

As an actor, you have to find some connection with your character, and if you don't take the side of the character you're playing, it's very hard to be convincing. It's no good imitating people; we have to find that kin quality in the self. Laurence Olivier, one of the most courageous actors of the century, said that if you play a murderer, you mustn't imitate the murderer, you must find the murderer in yourself.

The director is the advocate for all the characters. Directing makes you very understanding because you are dealing with a lot of people and you see what their problems are. It requires great energy, but it offers great creative opportunity. Since I've become one myself, I understand the demands made on the director, and when I am present as an actress at rehearsals, I now behave like an angel!

In the late sixties, a Franciscan brother and I teamed up to create something called the Everyman Street Theater Company. Its central concept was that anybody could become a member just by wanting to—with no auditions, no tryouts. Having decided that we would never leave anybody out, we had casts of literally hundreds of people. We worked in impoverished neighborhoods, but our final street date was always by the fountain at Lincoln Center. One day, one of the kids looked around at these palatial theaters and said to me, "Who owns this place?" And I said, "You do!" He was amazed to hear this, and when he was older he told me that this piece of news had changed his whole idea of possibilities in his future, and the future itself.

Feminism? It's a must. There is no alternative to it. We can't go back. We won't. I have seen in my lifetime the women's movement make a great improvement in women's lives in their homes and in workplaces, even though, of course, there should be much greater improvement. Mrs. Aquino has done more for feminism in the last ten years than anyone I can think of. And there are many other brilliant and courageous women blazing trails. If it's true that it has proved to be much more difficult to go forward than anybody thought, I believe it could be partly because of biological aspects and partly because women living alone don't take advantage of the resources around them in the way men do. Many of us are like the kid at Lincoln Center—we don't use the cultural and exercise centers available to us all. We need the confidence to accept our rights.

My forty-year-old marriage is very successful because my husband and I are extremely different, and consequently we augment each other's lives. Of course, there is a percentage of luck, too. There was everything against our ever meeting, but we, so to speak, "recognized" each other on sight and have never willingly been apart since.

In general, my view of life is nearly always optimistic. In an unhappy situation I think I would always try to do everything I could to change or improve it. I don't have much resignation.

People get locked into life because they have not thought of an alternate. You can't have choice until you know there is something else to choose. Some people don't ever come around to that. But once you realize there is an alternative, you can make great strides.

As an actor, I want to connect with an audience, to communicate something of truth and value about human beings. If that sounds pretentious, it must be understood that it's very difficult to talk about art because it's something you have to experience. It's like religion. People can talk about religion, but it's almost impossible for others to understand their meaning. However, if they were to say, "Go out and take care of others," and we all *did* that, perhaps religion might become more understandable. Anyway, that's the only way I can understand art. By performing it. Or helping others perform it. By doing it.

So let all of us do it, whether it's you or Martha Graham or Picasso, in whatever the art form, let us do it because we like it, and let that be enough.

Vickie Singer

I've gone through my husband's murder so many times that it almost gets to seeming like a staged play.

My daughter Charlotte was looking out the window with binoculars, watching John come up the lane from the mailbox. She screamed, "Mama, they're getting Daddy." I saw John surrounded by men. The fear went clear through me. I ran to get my boots and his rifle. Then I heard a shot. Charlotte witnessed what happened: John turned, took two or three running steps toward home, and then all of a sudden reared backwards. Blood shot out of his mouth, and he fell on his face on the ground. The police shot him right in the back.

By the time I got my boots on and got out there, they had grabbed his body, thrown him in the truck, and started heading down the road. Shirley, Heidi, Timothy, and I were four abreast, running down the road. I had a rifle, Timothy had a BB gun, Heidi had a bow and arrow, and Shirley had a pistol.

There was a great big pool of blood with his hat right on top of it. It was just horrid. We froze in our tracks. I think I swore, I really do. Heidi was yelling, "You cowards." Shirley and I started crying and holding each other.

Back up at the house, the sheriff called me and said the police shot John and they took him to the hospital. My thoughts almost stood in midair. He said they wanted to take the family in and they wanted us to come peaceably. All I could think of was my husband. They came and they took me and the children to the juvenile detention center. They lied to me and told me that they would take me to see my husband. Instead a policeman drove me to the Salt Lake County Jail. They handcuffed me. They made me take my hair out of a bun. This real tough,

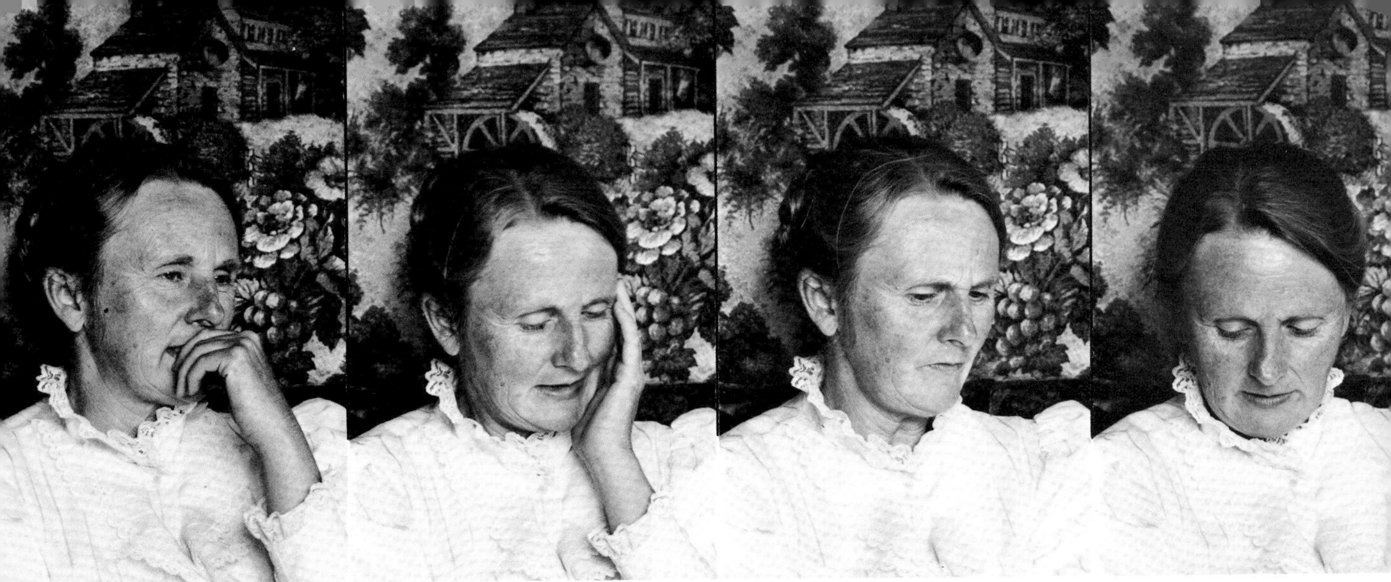

uncompassionate-as-heck-looking matron frisked me. I felt so utterly pitiful.

I'd never been in a jail. They had to walk me through these men's quarters, and this matron had a gun, and the guys, the way they look at you—I felt like I was in hell. They put me in this cell: one little cot, mattress on the floor, a toilet, a sink.

They came in and told me my husband was dead. To hear that—it's like you're falling down a time chamber and you can't hear quite well. It's just like you're under ether, you're in a well. I started crying, "Oh John, oh John." I said, "He can't be dead."

Sometimes you think, Is this life real? Or is this just a play? It sounds like the biggest fictionalized story you could think of, but it's not.

What happened to John and me involves all of us. When you stand on what you truly believe for your life, it affects other lives, too. We weren't some religious fanatics over in the corner of the hills. It doesn't matter what religion I am. It matters what happened in America, when people stood on the constitutional and religious freedoms. That's what this story is all about.

My real, true life started—as far as what I feel was my path in life—when I met John. John was a self-sufficient, handsomely rugged type mountain man. He built this log cabin with his bare hands. He was the hardest worker I've ever heard tell of, a Paul Bunyan type. He lived by faith and hard work.

My family and townsfolk believed that I was nuts for marrying my husband. There had been a lot of prejudice against John in the community because he was German. John's father was a Nazi, but not John. Prejudice had built up because of his strong religious beliefs. He was labeled a religious fanatic or a rebel.

I guess I was what you would call popular when I was growing up. I was a tap dancer and a twirler; I was the head of a really snappy twirling drill team. I was the homecoming queen, and then I won the Summit County queen contest. It didn't go to my head, though; I wasn't really that interested. But everyone acted as if I was their property and John, who was twelve years my senior, was robbing them. They thought he must have hypnotized me. The problem became so intense that my parents were going to put me in a mental institution. They were going to arrest John for kidnapping.

I knew from deep within that I was supposed to marry John—like you know your name. Without a doubt in the world. We went up into Oregon and eloped. We sealed our marriage through time and eternity in the Mormon Temple three months after our elopement.

It was the only time I had defied my parents' wishes. I respected them, was

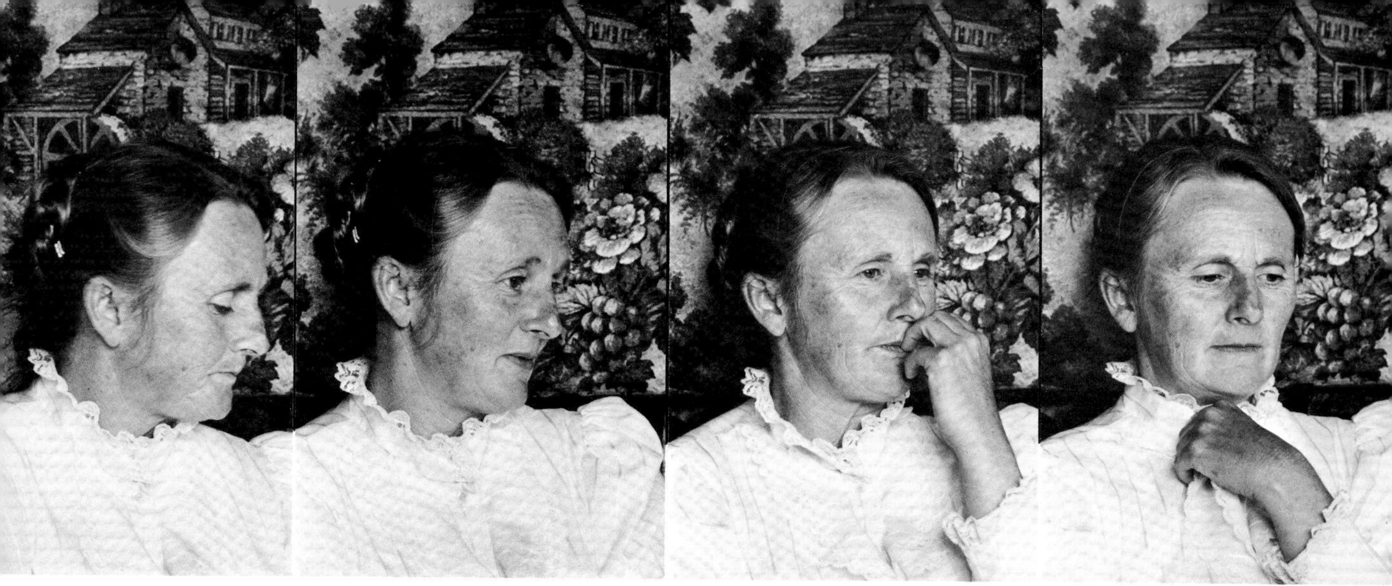

close to my mother. My father is a boilermaker. I think that in a way John was kind of a father image because I was never close with my father. I have a younger brother and sister. We really didn't do much as a family together, but I think I was happy.

From the time John and I were married, I felt that we had been together forever. It was so right, so right. I thought, How can my mother be so unhappy when I am so happy? I wanted her to know, but she told me I had stabbed her in the back.

My mother can't tolerate my beliefs. She feels I am brainwashing my children. My oldest daughter, Heidi, is twenty-two. My second daughter, Suzanne, is twenty-one. My boy, Timothy, is almost twenty.

John and Vickie

My youngest daughter, Charlotte, is eighteen, Joseph is fifteen, Benjamin thirteen, and Israel is ten.

I really wanted to have a large family. People were concerned because they thought we were having too many children too close together. We do not believe in the pleasure of the sexual act without the responsibility of the offspring. We were dedicated to having children and raising them up to God, always joyously awaiting the arrrival of our next little child. John was a loving and responsible father.

We were such a close family. We didn't have a lot of money, but we enjoyed our life. We taught our children that there are things you do and things you don't do. Temper tantrums or talking back were unheard of. We were firm, and they knew what was expected. The girls were trained to sit properly and keep their legs together so you couldn't see up their dresses—you know, the regular manners. They didn't get beat, but they got a good spanking sometimes. We didn't have a lot of friends because people didn't understand. They felt we were rather peculiar.

We have held to the early teachings or the fundamentals of the Mormon church. There are so many things they are teaching now that are just totally opposite to what they were teaching in the early days. We don't believe that you

Vickie with daughters, Charlotte and Heidi

can compromise or modernize the Gospel, the commandments of God. Truth is truth. We were ridiculed for simply taking the Scriptures literally, accused of disobedience to Church doctrine, and excommunicated from the Mormon Church in 1972.

In 1973 we took our children out of public school. We felt that it was our religious and moral responsibility to raise our children in the proper environment, and we felt that the public school was taking them away from the better education that we were providing here at home.

The schools seemed to take control of our children. The little children went to school on the bus at 8:30 and didn't get home until 4:00. It seemed like home was just a dropping-off place. Sometimes at school boys would look up my daughters' dresses—the girls wore longer dresses that I made them—and try to see their underwear, and that would upset my girls. There were other things—the year that we took Heidi out of school, nine girls in the senior class had to get married because they were pregnant.

One day, John saw Martin Luther King portrayed beside George Washington as a great patriarch in one of the kid's textbooks. He said Martin Luther King was a Communist-inspired rabble-rouser and didn't believe he should be put up there next to the great father of our country. It wasn't because the guy was black, in particular, but everybody picked up on that and said, "You are a racist." John didn't hate the blacks, but we believe we should stay to our own race as far as marrying.

The textbook was showing intermingling of the races, and John felt this was the onslaught of mongrelization. You can see our concern as far as our religious beliefs.

So my husband took our children out of school. It is a question of who has the rights over children—the state or their parents? John knew his constitutional and religious rights, and he believed in them, full force. The superintendent told us he would probably have to press charges and refer us to the juvenile court.

John built a schoolhouse and taught the older children reading, writing, arithmetic, and religion, and I taught the smaller children their ABC's and colors. We had a shorter school day—two to three hours. After lunch the children would have time to do their hobbies—building wooden toys, making sock dolls, finding Indian artifacts. John and I taught them how to take care of the home, take care of animals, garden. I taught them how to sew, how to cook, how to measure. We were teaching our children in such a practical way. It's wonderful to learn something and apply it. I feel that sometimes the schools waste a person's time. To dissect a frog in biology—I can't remember all those things, and I haven't used any of it.

We were always engaged in something that was educational, that was helping them be their own person, their own self. This was our goal: to have self-sufficient, independent, God-fearing, very morally clean children.

But the school board wanted us to follow a certain curriculum of theirs, and they wanted to supervise and test our children. They told John he would have to conform. We had to go to a psychologist and be tested. They found that my IQ was in the top 30 percent of women in the nation and John was in the top 8 percent of men in the nation.

Society was so concerned that we weren't able to handle our lives or that our children would suffer terribly, wouldn't be up with their peer group. In things we felt were most important in this life, I believe they surpassed their peer group. We didn't feel academics were first on the list of importance in building character but felt the children should have the basic skills to be able to deal with their lives. They didn't have to compete, because they were their own person. We're just free-thinking, free-feeling, independent individuals. But we were looked down upon because we believed and we lived accordingly. If we had lived a hundred years ago, we wouldn't have been persecuted the way we were.

When the school board came to test,

Joseph Singer

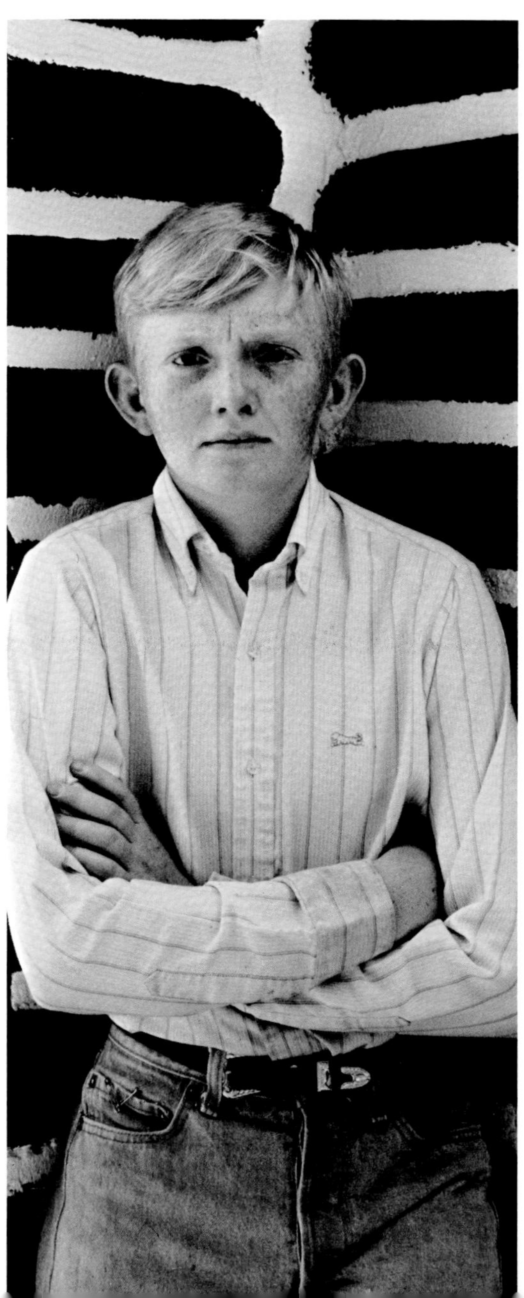

Vickie's granddaughter

the children didn't do too well. They weren't familiar with these kinds of tests. It was ridiculous. Their IQ scores were just so low. These tests were not competent in any way to measure a person's mental capacity. The psychologist made it sound as if our children were brain damaged. I used to let it bother me when they were calling my kids stupid, saying this and that, but I have made myself completely free of that. One night when I prayed about it, peace came over me. These big, intelligent psychologists didn't have the spirit of God within them to discern the proper thing about our raising our children. We didn't believe that the Lord said by this age you have to know that, by this age you have to know this. We didn't really care about their standards and qualifications they had set up for us.

The juvenile court gave us another year to prove ourselves. By this time we were fed up. This was in 1976, the Bicentennial year, and that good old spirit of 1776 came into me and John so strong. We agreed that the next time the fella called to test our children, we would refuse. We were sick to the core of having them look over our shoulders, peer down our necks, and tell us what to do with our children. They had made us slaves in our own home. My childrens' lives were my and my husband's business. We were going to reclaim the liberties that our forefathers fought and died for.

In 1977 we were summoned to court and accused with neglect of our children because we refused to send them to school. We went before the court about five times. They bartered over our children as if they were cattle, as if we didn't have anything to do with them. The state has more jurisdiction over the children than the parents. They tried to get us to bend, but we knew we did not have to compromise our constitutional or our religious freedoms.

The last time we were in court the judge told us if we would not compromise he would be forced to take our children away and put us in jail. We knew if we were to show up in the next court that we would have our children taken away, and so we stayed home. We sent three witnesses in our behalf to present a written statement specifying the reasons we felt we could not appear, but John was charged with contempt, and they put out a bench warrant for his arrest. We were on this property, under siege, for thirteen months.

There was a fervor to get John—almost as if they were pursuing a hardened criminal. Our house shook sometimes their darn surveillance airplane came so low. There were vehicles going around looking up here. They had binoculars. They would talk about us on the TV. The governor was planning to send an armored tank in here to shoot tear gas through our windows. They considered poisoning our water. John said he would never be the aggressor, but he carried a gun in the defense of property, family, and liberties.

You might say, Why did we go to that extreme, why didn't we compromise a little bit? I'll tell you why—because we knew with every fiber of our inner souls that we were to stand on our rights, constitutional and God-given. People thought we were just fanatics, I guess. It was hard to get across how deeply dedicated we were, knowing how we were supposed to live our lives.

Right at the time we were being tried by the state, plural marriage came into our lives. In our religion, plural marriage is considered morally superior to one marriage. It's really hard to explain to people who don't understand the Gospel as we believe it. But we are not ashamed of our beliefs. Two of my daughters are married to the same husband. John took another wife, not for his own personal lust or desire but because we both knew by testimony that Shirley was to be in our family. Our life's mission is not for the flesh, it's for the spirit.

People who had been on our side fell off like flies. They said Singer blew it good then. It was the test of the world, of the century! Oh my, if you want to do some soul-searching, plural marriage will do it. It's the ultimate overcoming of selfishness, jealousy, things that don't enhance a person's character. But it is a beautiful thing when you can subdue that little mortal ego self and the true you can come out. I learned to share my husband with Shirley, whom I love and respect.

I had a great struggle in overcoming jealousy and selfishness; I never dreamed it would be that hard. I think it's harder on the first wife, in some ways. I felt like I was a baby and kept falling down, trying to learn to walk and toddle. Insecure feelings just overwhelmed me. One time I got up in the middle of the night and I was crying and crying. I said to John, "How can you love two wives?" And John said to me, "Do you love only one of your children?" It was so beautiful how he explained it to me. I felt like a little girl sitting in his lap, crying. He said he was the luckiest man in the world to have two wonderful wives and that he didn't care how many wives he might have, he would never want to be without me. He promised me that no one would ever move me out of my place. He was trying to be patient, and the poor guy, I think it really was hard on him, too.

Vickie's daughter, Charlotte

John tried to be completely fair—it's supposed to be fifty-fifty with each wife—but it was hard for him under the circumstances. He was on constant guard because of the surveillance. He would spend one day and evening here and then one day and evening over with Shirley. She and I were really close friends. We kept busy teaching the children school. It was working out very well even though it was a trying time.

The lack of understanding we had to bear up under was unspeakable! It just looked like we were plum loco. At this point, I learned you can't care how other people judge you. We are individuals, and we have different callings in life. I have hoped to have the respect of other people in my beliefs, but I have not attained that. And so I have learned to live with it.

When I was in jail after John was killed, they sent in a psychiatrist to see if I was suicidal. He said, "How are you feeling?" I said, "How would you feel if your wife had been killed and you were put in jail and your kids were taken away?" I tell you, then he knew I wasn't any nut. I was just left there to bawl my eyes out, and boy did I. I walked around that cell in circles. I thought, How can I bear this without my children? I never felt such heartbreak in my life. I had been sentenced to thirty days without bail.

The public outcry against the state officials about John's death was so bad they could not keep me in jail. I was able to stay in the foster home where the children had been assigned and to see them the next day. Their hearts were just crushed to pieces. We were praying three times a day just to have strength to go on. Here our daddy is killed, and our hearts broken. We had to stay there for eight days before we could come home. We had John's funeral in Salt Lake City, and then we brought him up here to be buried.

It was so hard to come home. Everything looked strange, felt strange. We'd get up in the morning and have to face it all over again that John had been killed. The reaction that I had was very peculiar —I was actually upset because he didn't write or call me! We did have comforting dreams. His spirit stayed with us a long time. There is such a thin veil between life and death.

I knew I had to bring a wrongful death suit against the state in order to try to bring the truth forth, but our grievance was not redressed. My case has been thrown out of the federal court, the district court, and the U.S. Supreme Court. Had my lawyer, Gerry Spence, been able to take this to trial, it would have blown the lid off the state. But the power structure has tentacles everywhere—like an octopus. The officials who were involved in John's death are still going to have to answer. Those court records will not be lost. It was conspiracy to murder my husband.

I love the truth that America is supposed to stand for, but I find it a great hypocrisy. Home of the brave, land of the free—really? We put it to the test, and it isn't true! We weren't trying to push our beliefs on anybody else, just doing what we truly, deeply believed. America may sound good and look good on the out-

OUR
BELOVED
HUSBAND-FATHER
JOHN
JAN. 6, 1931 - JAN. 18, 1979
DIED A MARTYR FOR TRUTH
AND CONSTITUTIONAL FREEDOM

side, but the things she was founded on are corroded. When Independence Day comes around, I can't even celebrate it. It's blasphemy, utterly, mockingly, sickening to me. Something is terribly wrong in this country. There are a lot of injustices going on, where lives are being smashed by the powers that be. Our story is just one of them.

But I know John's death was not in vain. Two days before he was killed, John said to a news reporter, "Either way I will have gained the victory." It's true. We won the victory. They did not force my children back into public school.

My children are intelligent and responsible. It's been hard to raise and teach them myself. I've gone down to the bare basics—the three R's. They might be—to use a biblical phrase—unlearned in the ways of the world and somewhat academically, but as far as being able to cope with what they need to cope with, they are doing fine.

In terms of my independence and strength from within, nothing has changed since John's death. I live up here with my neighbors hating me and trying to get rid of me. But this is my home. My husband built this place. I lost him, and if I were to leave this home I feel I would be losing him again. I just know this is where we belong.

Hardness has built up over the years because our ways are just not acceptable. The pressures of being different! The neighbors think that John was destroyed because of his wickedness. My mother sent a thank-you note to the guy who killed him. People are so narrow-minded in these small communities—they get to thinking there is only one way to live or think or believe. If I were that narrow-minded I hope somebody would slap me in the side of the head.

When I look back at all that I have been through, I feel very strong. In July, 1984, my son Timothy had his accident. He was up cutting trees for firewood, and he cut this wedge out of a tree. He saw the way it was falling, turned around, and started walking away. He said it was just like a truck hit him in the back. It smashed his vertebrae into his spinal cord. He almost died there. He found out three weeks after his accident that he was permanently crippled.

Just after it happened, I was heartbroken and cried out to the Lord, "Oh, my poor boy." Then I was reminded of the Scripture—"In everything give thanks, for this is the will of God in Christ Jesus concerning you." I just gritted my teeth together and said, "Thank you God for Timothy's crippledness." And I thought it was the biggest lie I ever said. I had to work with myself. I just said, "Thank you, thank you," and early in the morning a real peace came over me. The peace of God passeth all understanding.

While Timothy was in the hospital, my son-in-law went up in the woods and got the wedge from the tree and fixed it for Timothy, to dedicate it to the glory of God, to give thanks for all things. Timothy had the wedge in the hospital—quite a piece of history right there.

I figure we've made it this far, and I figure we will make it the rest of the way. I have learned to cope with pressures that almost squeeze the air out of your lungs. But I know my life has a purpose. I know my husband will be resurrected, and I will be with him throughout eternity. I know there will come a time when Christ will reign on earth, and we will be a theocracy. No one can tell me different, because I know it.

People say, "If you had it to do over again, would you do the same?" Yes. I wouldn't change anything because I made every step a matter of prayer. On something that is a matter of principle or truth I just cannot compromise. When I am standing on something that I know is right and I have so much darn trouble, it's almost like a barometer—I know I am standing on the right thing.

In January 1988, Vickie Singer, her son-in-law Addam Swapp (husband of Vickie's daughters Heidi and Charlotte), and thirteen family members barricaded themselves on their property following Swapp's and Singer's alleged involvement in the bombing of a nearby Mormon church. The thirteen-day standoff with law enforcement officials ended in the death of one police officer. Addam Swapp was seriously wounded.

712
"Closings to Date"
"ATTITUDE
Is Everything"
And whatever you ask for
in prayer, having faith and
really believing, you will
receive.
Matthew 21:22
You do not have
because you do not ask.
James 4:2
Incentive Program
to May 9
% incr
$ increas
1. Lucille
2. Ann
3. Karen
1. Lucille
2. Ann
3. Karen

"Mo" Anderson

A lot of people think that the American Dream is dead. I don't believe that for one minute. If all the wonderful things that have happened to me can happen to a tenant farmer's daughter from Oklahoma, America, they can happen to anybody. My official title is Vice-President of Merrill Lynch Realty, in charge of the Edmond, Oklahoma, operation.

I'm not different from anybody else. I am convinced that no matter whether it's on a wheat farm in Oklahoma or a ghetto in New York City, if you are willing to pay the price—willing to work very hard—then you can achieve whatever you want to achieve.

I was born on a farm in northern Oklahoma, near Enid—a town that has the largest grain elevator space in the world. My parents were very, very poor. I grew up bathing in a little bitty washtub, and I didn't have an indoor bathroom until I was a sophomore in high school. My clothes were made out of feed sacks. It was exciting to go to the feed store with my father and choose the sacks of grain, because those sacks became my clothes.

My family moved around to several different farms, all in Oklahoma. Some of them were pretty run-down. I remember my mother taking cotton tea towels and chasing out the flies and gnats. We didn't have much, but, honey, what we had was clean.

I was the youngest of five children, the baby of the family. My parents couldn't afford me, and they didn't want another child. I was strictly an accident. That's why I have strong feelings about abortion: if my mother had been a contemporary woman, I probably wouldn't have had a chance to live, and it would have been terrible if I hadn't lived! There would have been a whole lot of people who would have missed something!

My father had a fourth-grade education, but he was very wise. He was really an inspiration to me. I would often watch him give away our last dollar to someone who needed it maybe worse than we did. It bothered me as a child to see him do that. But then he'd pat me and love on me a little bit and say, "The good Lord is just gonna meet our needs and don't you worry," and sure enough our needs would be met.

There was such a contrast between my mother and my father. My mother talked a lot about being poor. She told me they would never be able to send me to college. My dad told me over and over as a child, "You can do anything when you grow up—if you are willing to pay the price." I chose at a very young age to believe my dad.

Learning to work was the name of the game. When I was twelve years old, I would be up plowing in the fields before dawn during the busy harvest season, and I plowed until way after dark when the moon was bright enough. I was my father's boy in terms of the chores and duties. I didn't have time to cook and sew.

My mother canned all the fruits and vegetables, which we stored in the cellar for our food supply. Daddy would butcher a calf, and we had a smokehouse. We were never hungry. We'd have breakfast feasts of biscuits and gravy and eggs and sausage. I would be rewarded for good grades with lemon meringue pie. Our reward system was based on food because food was oftentimes the only thing my parents could give. If we had lived in a big city and hadn't had the garden, we might have been like New York City ghetto people.

Several years ago I became involved in a project trying to help poor people in an area east of here. While I was working to

"Mo" offers real estate advice on a weekly radio show.

help change attitudes and find jobs, everybody else in the project was just trying to get more government handouts. I finally just threw up my hands in despair because those poor people didn't need handouts. They needed to learn to work. The fact that I learned to work as a child was my salvation.

My job at a very young age—six or seven—was to go after the cattle in the evening. That pasture lane was where I did my dreaming. I would pretend that I was a musician performing in Carnegie Hall or that I was a bride walking down the aisle of a big cathedral. It was in that pasture lane that I made a determination that I absolutely was not going to be poor when I grew up. I was determined to work hard, become successful, and make my life count.

I learned at a young age that people would respect me for who I was and what I was and not how much I had. Even though I often felt inferior and intimidated when I was growing up, I still achieved. I was a leader in my little classes in school. I was a cheerleader, I excelled musically, I sometimes got the leads in plays. Even though I never felt quite like I truly belonged in the inner circle, I was allowed to join because the ones who were in it knew I was good.

A small college here in Oklahoma offered me a scholarship, so I went there my first year. Then I transferred to the University of Oklahoma. I didn't have a scholarship, so I started borrowing money. I repaid every penny. I worked almost full-time, carried a full load, and it was very hard. Richard, who was my boyfriend at the time, helped me. Education was my ticket: I knew that if I worked hard and played hard and fought hard that I could make it someday. Whatever "make it" means.

Back when I was growing up, financial freedom meant having running water and an indoor bathroom. It meant doing the grocery shopping without worrying that you would exceed x number of dollars. I still get excited when I shop for groceries without a list, buying whatever I want. I relish those things. I have not allowed myself to take them for granted. I still get a thrill out of the icemaker in my refrigerator.

I bought a Cadillac a few years ago. It had push-button everything. And I was so uncomfortable with that stupid car for the first couple weeks, because I had always identified Cadillacs and Lincolns with rich people, and I don't see myself as rich. Rich is relative. But I grew accustomed to the car and, you know, I still get a kick out of my power windows!

There are some real adjustments that you have to make when you have a bit of a poverty complex. When you can't have

"Mo" and Richard

something and you want it, and then you can have it and you want it, you kind of go crazy for a little while. I am still like a little kid in a candy store, wanting things, but I am not as bad as I used to be.

I struggled with guilt when we bought things we didn't really need—like these diamond rings of mine. They are nothing compared to what the girls in New York buy, but they were a big deal to me. I struggled—I shouldn't really have them. I thought about all the poor people who needed things. I am still struggling with that fine line of enjoying blessings without being extravagant. I never had any of these things growing up. There is a real secure feeling in knowing that if I lost every material thing I had, I would survive just fine. Richard is not into material things at all. He is a good balance for me.

Richard is the love of my life. We were high school sweethearts. Prior to our junior year in college, we married, which was really crazy, because we were much too young. Those first years were so hard. We had very little money, and three months after we were married, I became pregnant. We were barely mature enough to be married, much less parents. Now I'm thrilled, because we have two wonderful children, but oh my, at the time.

Our lives were further complicated by Richard's long battle with depression. We didn't know if his depression was physical or emotional and, in the early years of our marriage, didn't have the money to find out. Many times he didn't have enough mental energy to go around, and he would withdraw. I thought that maybe I was the cause of the depression, and my own fears of rejection surfaced. I felt so alone. I was outgoing and loved to be around people, and he was quiet and reserved. I saw him as kind of a little gem and thought he just needed to be polished. I thought I would polish him. *Wrong!*

I can remember living three blocks

away from the school where I taught sixth grade. Walking down block number one, I often cried my eyes out because I just didn't know how to cope. I thought, I can't stand to live the rest of my life like this. But I love him and I think he is such a beautiful person and I'll feel like a real rat if I call it quits. On block number two, I would wipe the tears from my eyes and powder my nose. Block number three probably had the greatest effect on my life of anything. On block number three I practiced acting like I was happy, so that when I reached that school door nobody would know how I hurt on the inside. I will never forget the morning I discovered—maybe six years later—that I wasn't acting anymore. I really *was* content and happy. I realized I could learn to be happy even when the circumstances in my life weren't so great. And that's what I made a conscious decision to do—to be happy in my life, even though Richard's depression and our financial difficulties didn't get any better for a long time.

Our problems caused me to learn that I needed help from a higher source. My Christian faith is really important to me. I believe that Christ is the Son of God, my friend and Lord, and my salvation. I believe that He did live and die and that He paid the price for the sins of crummy mankind. I don't have the rest of it figured out and frankly I don't care. I get sick of people arguing, "Do you sprinkle or do you immerse?" What is important is that we treat people with respect all week long. It doesn't matter if we occupy

a pew in a church on Sunday. What are our lives really like? That's what counts.

In 1974 we moved to Edmond. We quit going to the shrinks and psychologists we'd been trying and instead went to an internist. We learned that Richard's depression was basically a chemical imbalance. The medication he received made a huge difference. Although he will still have some blue days from time to time, he is doing well now.

I tell you, I am so glad we made it! He's just like a rose that is unfolding, becoming all God wants him to be. I wouldn't trade what I have with him now for anything in the world. I am grateful for our problems, because they taught me the greatest lesson of my life: my happiness is not dependent on any other person. I had to walk that third block many times to discover on my own that I could be happy regardless of the circumstances. Learning to be happy and fulfilled and feeling good about myself on the inside are the things that laid the foundation for the successes I have experienced in the business world.

Richard is the one who encouraged me to get into real estate, by enrolling me in a real estate class. He said, "You're a real good teacher and you know how to teach, but now it's time to move on and learn some other things." I loved being a teacher and I was fulfilled in my career. My impression of realtors wasn't exactly positive. I thought they drove Cadillacs, Mercedes, and Lincolns, made lots of money, and weren't really interested in people; they just wanted their commissions. In fact, when I thought of real estate, I thought of a mediocre building with a sign that said, "Real Estate, Fish Bait, and Insurance." I had "stinkin' thinkin'" in my mind regarding the profession!

But Richard had such strong feelings about it that we took a real estate class in Ponca City, America, and he tutored me because I didn't know the difference between a mortgage and a deed. I got the lowest possible score you could get and still pass the test! Richard, oh shoot, he aced it!

So I entered the real estate business and was never more miserable in my life. I cried almost every night for about six months, and I did not make one penny. Well how could I? I had such a bad attitude. One night, in my prayers, I said, "Lord, I am so miserable that I cannot possibly be in your will, whatever your will is. If you want me to stay in this business, would you please give me three sales during the month of August as a sign?"

Asking for three sales during August of 1974, with my attitude and background, was like asking for a miracle. I don't

believe in playing games like that with God, but I was so desperate I did it. To make a long story short, at 11:45 p.m. on August 31, I had my third sale.

After that I began to be successful because I had a decent attitude. During the first six months, I hadn't made a dime. The second six months I did a million in volume and I generated $17,000 in income which isn't that big of a deal, but it was a real big deal to me.

With less than a year of experience, I began to dream of having our own company. I pulled in two more experienced gals, Ruth and Jerry, and we started our company in approximately 300 feet of space, with a typewriter, a few desks, and that's about all. We were really green about what it took to build a company.

The first five years were terribly difficult. I sold a little bit, but I also did everything else. I helped recruit agents, trained them, and organized the office. I'd never had a business course in my life, but I seemed to have a natural ability. We began to grow.

All my work was to build the best brokerage firm in town, because I'm very competitive. I wanted the people who worked for us to be proud. I never dreamed we would become so financially successful.

Many of my competitors do not understand why I am so successful because they can see that I don't know a whole lot about the technical aspects of real estate. When I have time to read, I don't read real estate books. I read people books. I want to learn more about people interacting. Richard and I go into a bookstore and look at the self-help books to see if there is anything we haven't read, and if there is, we buy it.

Shoot, I don't know how to put certain trades together and I don't intend to learn! If I need to put a trade together I push the buttons on my phone and call somebody who can tell me how to do it. What I know a lot about is people. Some of my competitors don't think that's important, but that's the most important thing of all!

In 1981 we began to have people call us up and ask if we wanted to sell our business. When you work hard to build a company, you consider it your little baby. You want to turn it over to someone who is going to nurture it and care about it as much as you do. You see, I really love the people in our company. I had a feeling that there was real integrity in the Merrill Lynch organization, and so we sold the company to them. It was my first time to ever deal with a corporate entity, and I have been extremely pleased. We were blessed with a great buy-out.

I am one of the lucky ones, because I love my boss. At first, we were wary of

one another. I am certain he wondered if I could become a real team player after being an owner for ten years. One day after a meeting I said to him, "I just wanted to tell you how glad I am that they made you my boss." And then I looked at him and said, "I want you to know that I am committed to being one of your best employees. A team player." He melted like a piece of butter on a hot stove! Now I never tell him my opinion on anything unless he asks. When he asks, I tell him everything. We have a wonderful relationship and he thinks I hung the moon and I just love him and his little wife, too.

At the end of my contract with Merrill Lynch I'll have to decide what I will do next. I am seriously considering consulting as a possibility. I am discovering that a lot of the theories behind our business apply to many other kinds of businesses. You learn some basic principles of living from business situations because you deal with conflict and differences of opinion. It's a real challenge to me to see how quickly I can get people through their hostility and get them smiling. I use diplomacy.

I have a real difficult time identifying with leaders of the women's movement, like Gloria Steinem, because I think they are absolutely taking the wrong approach. It's a real contradiction that I do so many things that feminists espouse, but I am not one of them. Some of the feminists on the media just sound bitter, hard, and harsh to me; they come on like a bulldozer. They've helped to create a head-on situation so the little gal who is being pinched on the rear by her boss is having an even harder time because many men are retaliating against the movement.

I'd like to teach some of these feminists how to use manipulation. You can use manipulation for good, or you can use it for bad. And men, for the most part, are very easily manipulated. I manipulate men quite often. They don't realize they are being manipulated because I am very good at it. But I am very conscientious about using this technique to create a win-win situation for me and a win-win situation for them. If feminists would do it my way, I believe they would get to the top a lot faster.

I haven't encountered male chauvinism towards me. Many career women do encounter some grief along the way. It's my opinion that if a woman has a problem with men coming on to her, wanting to go to bed with her, that quite possibly it's *her* problem. Women tend to send out vibes that invite men to do what they do. A woman's attitude can certainly make the difference.

I think that any woman who really has the desire to be the corporate executive, or whatever she wants to be, can be just that. But a price has to be paid for success—and the price I paid wasn't forty hours a week.

I almost always work a twelve-hour day and then often bring a full briefcase home with me. I do that at least six days a week, and that's better than it used to be. Back when we owned the company, especially during the early years, I would say on the average of two times a week I would get to the office at 7:30 a.m. and not leave until 2 a.m. There is no free lunch in anything you do.

I just want to encourage *all* people, men *and* women, because there seems to be an attitude in this country that you can't do anything unless you are wealthy or you have a rich uncle, and that is simply not true. At the end of each sales meeting, I have what I call an "inspirational time." Here's one story that I tell to illustrate a basic principle. See if you can see what it is.

There are two kinds of birds that fly over the California desert—the vulture and the tiny little hummingbird. The vulture with his outstretched wings will make his silent sweeping soar until he spots the carcass of some dead animal and will zero down upon it. In all the vast desert all the vulture sees is the carcass.

The hummingbird flies over the same desert, and he never sees the carcass. He spies the blossom on the cactus plant, spears it with his long, skinny bill, and sucks the honey from the bloom. Each creature sees what he is looking for.

If you want to look for the negative in our company or in your family or in your community, hey, you're gonna find it. But if you look for the positive, that's what you'll find. You have the choice. What are you going to look for with your customers, with your sellers, with your company? Are you going to be the vulture and love that carcass, or are you going to be that little hummingbird and get the honey from the bloom?

"Mo" poses next to a sign put up by Edmond residents in their tornado-demolished neighborhood.

Barbara Bane

Once in a while I think about what it would be like to have chosen a completely different life. I was an art history major in college—Renaissance architectural history. Later I ran a small art gallery, did some art consulting, did some archeology. Sometimes I wonder what it would be like to live in a little villa outside of Florence, studying architectural history. It almost wouldn't be work, almost like living a fantasy...but I don't know. To me, living in the real world is much more interesting.

I'm a sprinkler fitter, which is a specialized form of a pipe fitter. I pipe fire protection systems—fairly heavy-duty work, in a small, fairly specialized trade. There are about ten women sprinkler fitters in a union of maybe 500 to 600 men in my local.

About five years ago I was working fifty-hour weeks in the financial district here in San Francisco, doing computer work, supervising four or five people, and going home every night with knots in my stomach, overworked and underpaid. I thought, There has got to be a better way; this is for the birds. I think about the worst thing in the world is not to like your work. I figured, what the hell, and I went and applied for a lot of different jobs. I didn't want to work in an office.

I started my apprenticeship in the trade— a registered, four-year apprenticeship. You get training on the job, and you get paid. The teaching is visual and oral transmission, not a school-learning situation. After about six weeks I realized that I really liked it—loved working with my hands, liked being outside, loved the people I was working with.

People say, "You're a lesbian," or,

"You're a feminist, how can you stand working with all these men?" I happen to really like working with these men. I think construction workers are great. And I actually prefer their company to a lot of liberal white-collar men I know. They're very honest. They're up front, and if they don't like something, they'll let you know. They also have a great sense of humor.

Another thing I like about being a construction worker is that I don't have to look like Twiggy. I can remember spending years when I was growing up and in college thinking, You don't look like *Vogue* magazine, you're not a willowy thing, you're too muscular, you're too this, you're too that. I spent a long time trying to force myself into this mold of trying to look like someone else. Now I trust my body to do the things I want it to do. I enjoy muscles—on women and on men. They're very functional for what I do. I feel much more comfortable about my body now, both since I came out and I started doing this work.

When I became a tradeswoman, it was important to me not only to enjoy my work but to make a good living from it, too. There was definitely a shift in my life when I gave up thinking that I didn't mind living hand-to-mouth. There came a point when yes, I minded. I would much rather do something I enjoy and get paid for it. You don't have to be poor to accomplish things. Rita Mae Brown says you can do a lot more in this world with money. For one thing, money gives you one more way of helping other people.

Tradesmen make $28 an hour plus benefits, so it works out to about $35 an hour. You don't get paid if you don't work, but there's a great pension plan. How can you beat that? Where else can someone come out with a high school education and go through a program and make $40,000 a year? We have the union to thank for that. It's a hard way to make a living, but it pays well and it's a good job. I think I have the best of all possible worlds in my work situation—I really like what I do and I also make a decent living at it. What more could you want?

I can't say that the trades welcome women with open arms, but I didn't have too much trouble with open hostility. Some women do encounter that. Most of what you encounter is much more subtle. A woman has to prove herself. It's not like a man walking in on the job—you really have to do a little better, work a little harder. I think a woman that stays at the job has about ten times more perseverance than your average male, which really says something about her character.

There's still a lot of discrimination out there. I wish I could say that it's changed in the four and a half years that I've been doing this—since the time I was literally thrown out of a contractor's office

because he didn't want to deal with hiring women—but it hasn't. Most of the discrimination I encounter on a job site is not because I am a lesbian, it's because I am a woman.

The guy I worked with my first year and a half in the trade had a $100 bet going with another apprentice on the job that he could get me out of the trade in a week. We were doing a really messy outdoors job tying in a huge underground plastic pipe. He gave me this shovel and pointed to a ditch full of mud that went as far as you could see and said, "I want you to dig this ditch out." And I said, "OK." So that tactic didn't work. Eventually we became very close friends. He got kind of won over.

My experience has been that once men see that you are willing to do your share of the work and that you are fairly capable, they are pretty decent. The hardest thing for me was getting these guys to give me the training. There is more tendency with men to just send women off to do the busy work. I think men are taught at an earlier age to push, push, push for what they want. They don't have as many compunctions about stepping up and saying, "Let me do that." A little bit of bluster will carry you a lot further in this work than timidity, and a sense of humor helps.

It's also really nice to know that there are people out there you can talk to about what you do. I belong to a group called Trades-women, Inc., which is a support group for women in nontraditional trades. Sometimes you can feel kind of crazy. My hat's off to women who do this kind of work without a support group. I can imagine someone living out in the middle of nowhere, who doesn't know other women, maybe who's got a family and four or five kids to raise—it would be really hard. I don't think I could do that. Our group of 100 women does everything from giving conferences and editing a newsletter to monitoring unions in affirmative action. We have to keep constant tabs on things so that we don't lose ground.

My greatest fear is that we trades-women are going to become dinosaurs. The women in World War II, all the Rosie the Riveter types, just got told, "OK ladies, we don't need you anymore, bye." The women didn't feel there was a choice. I want a choice, want to see other women get into the trades. I don't want that option to disappear.

Men have been told their whole lives, "You can do this." Women don't have that. We have to step in and pick up this slack. The reason I am talking to you now is that it is important to me to tell other women that you can do this. I can do it, so you can do it too, because I am not out of the ordinary. Men aren't gonna tell us that. We have to tell each other. It's a gigantic pep talk: we can do it.

More and more women are finding a

way. If anything you can say or do or write or put in a picture—if that's a picture to another woman and it gives her just a little bit of encouragement, that's enough. We don't have to be islands in this.

I learned at a very young age that it's important to take part, and that means giving—for me, being political. How can you close your eyes to what's happening? Some political work I do because I'm gay, some because I'm a woman and a woman in a nontraditional field.

Many women who came before me worked very hard to make it possible for me to have this job, and I'm grateful. Some days I think it's a little miracle that I can do this job, because twenty years ago it wouldn't have been possible. It's important to give back that kind of thing—it's just what you owe.

The way we live our lives in this country is dependent upon people getting involved with one another and upon empowerment. The way you give yourself power in your life is to take charge and have some involvement in the things that affect your life. To give that up is, to me, really less than human.

Everything we do touches something else, human as well as inanimate. The nuclear movement is directly related to how we oppress the earth. If this is how we treat the lands, how we pollute and destroy, how will we treat people? If this is how we treat human beings, what the hell will we do to the earth? There is a direct correlation between how we treat things, a whole chain of beings, a link. Women have a little more idea of a link between all things, I don't know why that is.

One of the ideas I like most in the Bible is that we are put on earth as stewards of what's here. You don't need to be a totally political animal, and I don't think you have to devote your whole life to it, but I do think everybody owes a certain amount of time to the things they think are worth saving—it's like moral tithing. A lot of people think that things like citizenship and morality are cornball, but there is really nothing cornball about them. It's important that people be up front and speak up for good deeds, be good to other people and lead an honest, upright life.

We don't have to have God to have a notion of right and wrong. We should do things because they are right. Look at things from a human perspective. Do unto others as we would have them do unto us—that's a real human relation. How do I relate to you as another human being, not how do I relate to you through Christ? Why should we do things because of the promise of heavenly rewards? We should do them because it is the way to treat people here on earth. We should do them because it's good to do.

Most days I think the best thing that I can do is just be an example. It's good for the guys on the job to work next to a woman, for once, and see that she can do the job. That is worth as much as fifty million pamphlets I could pass out or fifty hours of arguing.

My experiences have really changed my father's mind about women and what women can do. And it has opened my parents' eyes to realize the things I have to deal with being gay. Before, they had a more pat idea of how the world went: if you work real hard then you get rewarded. That's not always the case. People in this country who don't happen to be white don't get the same breaks, let's face it. A lot of people struggle so much harder than someone like me. What I do

is not really hard compared to many people in this country. I'm a woman but essentially I've had all the breaks.

I grew up in a fairly middle-class family in Houston. Texas is home to me. I have all my old friends there, my family. Whether or not I like the people there, I understand those people, and I understand that place. Someone said to me once, "It's a geography that you understand in your heart."

I love living in San Francisco—it's beautiful, I like being able to ski and rock climb in a couple of hours, I like the anarchy of mass communication available here—but I still consider myself to be a Texan and a Southerner above all. I think the way we Southerners do manners is where we have one leg up on everyone else in the world. Manners make things flow smoother, they expedite the quality of life. Isn't that what social skills are about—making other people feel at ease and valued? Everybody in the South learns to flirt from an early age, almost like they eat, sleep, and breathe. A

sense of humor is like a natural extension of having learned at a very early age how to flirt. It's a joy to watch a master at work; Yankees are real susceptible. The problem with Southern manners is that you reach the point of diminishing returns, where they cease to make life easier and begin to cover up for things that need to be said. In the long haul it can make things harder.

I was pretty independent as a kid, a real little rebel type—you tell me I couldn't do something and I was damn well going to do it. It's been that way all my life—anything that's a challenge appeals to me. I have a younger sister who is the exact opposite of me—a sorority queen who did all the right things—and I have a brother who is about ready to go into a military career. We enjoy one another's company, but it hasn't always been easy to get along. Now we are seeing each other as adults and coming together as friends.

My parents are fairly old-fashioned Southerners, fairly conservative. They're

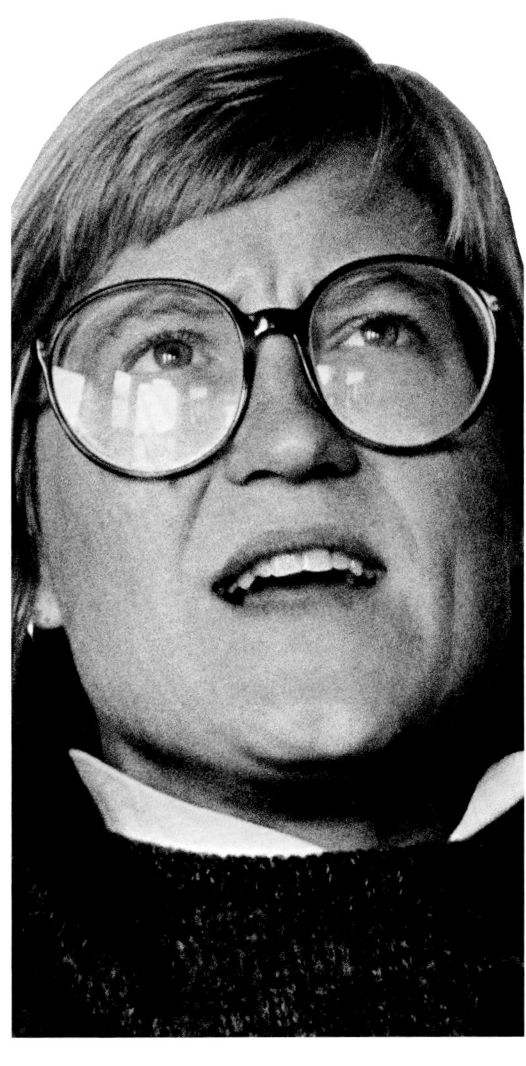

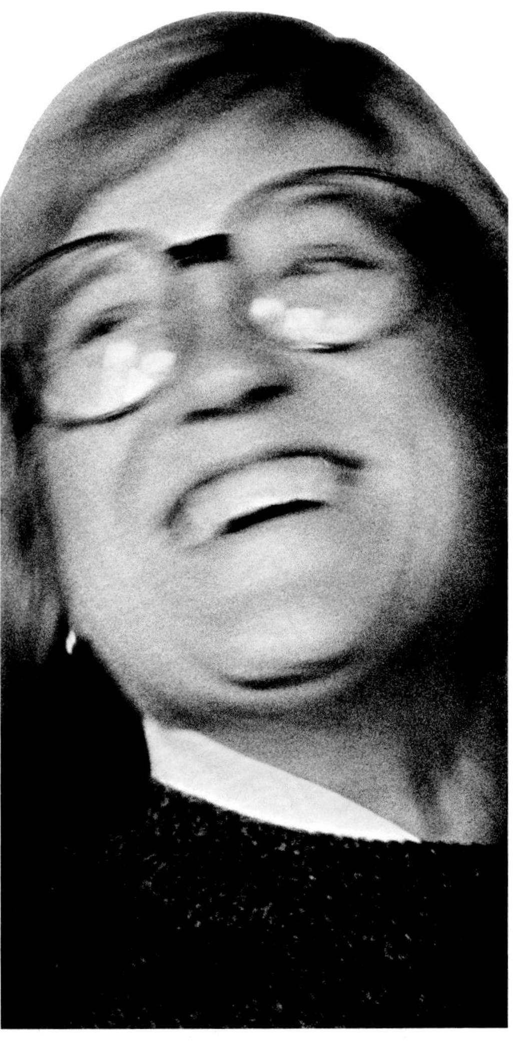

good people, very moral, very honest. They're not crazy about my being gay because they think it makes my life harder. And it does sometimes. Being a gay person is not easy, but I would never ever go back to being heterosexual. It's not important that your life be easy. It's important that you be happy and your life be interesting.

I was a very happy heterosexual for many years. I think I was twenty-two when I came out. It was the kind of thing where I woke up one morning and I just happened to have fallen in love with a co-worker and it was a woman, not a man. It was like someone had hit me on the head. You know, bam. It scared me to death. I left for Italy for an archeological dig two weeks later. I remember sitting on a patio out in the countryside the day that I got there thinking I have made a terrible, terrible, really terrible mistake—I'm running away from something. I cried and cried and it was too late. I didn't have the money to go home. It was stupid for me to run away from it. I decided I was gay.

I waited a couple of years to tell my parents. I was pretty nervous about it. I remember sitting at the table with them and saying to myself, At 6:30 I'm going to say this—and I made myself come out with it—but it went a lot better than I thought. They both were great. Their message was: we can't say we're crazy about this, but you're our daughter and we love you no matter what choices you make.

Most people in this world who do things that are different have to have something deep inside that they pull up on. You have to have a sense inside yourself that what you are doing is all right despite the validation of other people or lack thereof. How many other people have to buck something like that on a daily basis? Have to have that kind of willpower? That's overcoming a lot. It might make for a little stronger person, day to day. Maybe that's chauvinistic of me to think that. I think there are more healthy psychological survivors now, but if you think about what it means to be gay, even now, it's still an uphill battle. I was beat up in a homophobic attack and spent a year trying to track down the assailant. I'm a real solution-oriented person, and I found that trying to do something about it really helped to get rid of the anger. I don't focus on feelings, I focus on things I can do.

One of the ways human beings get by in the world is by trusting that we can find a way if we try hard enough. It may not always be the way we want, but some kind of way. I can never ever imagine any situation in life that would make me want to quit. There is always something you can do if you just try hard enough. I think it's a belief I got from my parents, and it has nothing to do with being a woman. It's just a sense that you can do whatever you want to do.

I can see going back to Texas from California when I'm older. I don't really think sprinkler fitting is the kind of thing I want to do when I'm forty-five years old. It's too hard. I think I'd like to be a labor lawyer—the law could use some rank and file people, and the unions could use some help...if unions are still around. It wouldn't be easy, going back to school at this point, but like I said before, Whoever asked that life be easy? It's not supposed to be easy. It's supposed to be good and it's supposed to be interesting.

Gloria Vadeboncoeur

Don't they say that your life is all mapped out for you? From the time you're born?

It's hard, living. I hate working in a shoe shop. I worked at the factory, this last time, it's going on twelve years. The first time I worked there five years.

You take a lot of shit working in a shoe shop. They don't share the work fair. They don't even want to give you your goddam paycheck. They wouldn't give you an hour off. They make you feel like a piece of shit. That's how I feel about it. I don't know how anybody else feels about it. They don't give you a Christmas party. You know how most places give you a turkey? Nothing, nothing. Let's face it: you spend more time in the shoe shop working than you do anything else. I hate it, I hate it. I really hate it.

But there isn't any choice, because if I don't work then we don't eat. I went back to work when my husband lost his leg. He was working at the paper mill when he got sick. He found out that he had arteriosclerosis—that's hardening of the arteries—premature. At age thirty-three. Severe blockage from the knee down. His other leg's no good either; it's deteriorating slow. High cholesterol buildup. The doctors told him to stop smoking, which he doesn't do. He smokes worse than ever.

After he got sick he couldn't work. The paper mill paid for all the bills and everything—the hospital bill was $30,000—but they were only giving him like $70 a week to live on, and there were the six of us. Welfare gave us $34 every two weeks, which was kind of lousy because how can you live on that? Disability—we've been on it for twelve years now—we had to wait a solid year before we could get on that.

So I just decided it was time for me to go back to work. I went to the factory because they knew me from before and because it always says Stitchers Wanted on a big sign outside of the shop. I had been a bottom cementer before. My grandmother was a fancy stitcher in a factory, and she made pretty good money, so I figured I'd give it a try. I didn't know anything else. I had quit school in my third year of high.

I think that I could have been a beautician; I give permanents. Basically I learned just by watching other people cut hair. But I don't feel as if I am smart enough—you have to go to school and learn all the things about the head, you know. I'll tell you, though, a shoe shop is a real sucky place to work.

I have cleared $225 a week—that's good time. I have to make $300 and some to clear $200 and some. Even so it's not enough. It's never enough. My husband and I both smoke cigarettes. That's two packs a day. And my husband drinks two six-packs a day. That's $70 a week out of my paycheck. I work just to feed us all. And I feel guilty going to bingo on Saturday night, spending $20! I earn it. I work hard for it, but bingo takes it away from other things.

I won the cover-all one time, and I got so excited I had an asthma attack. The next day I was totally sick. Thank God I had won that $591 because I was out of work for a week. I guess God does provide in some ways, doesn't He?

Basically, before my husband got sick, my life was pretty good. When he lost his leg everything changed. It hasn't been too happy in the last twelve years. When I was a kid growing up it was fine because I had my grandmother and I knew I was loved there at least. I've lived in Haverhill, Massachusetts, all my life, except for a year and a half in Exeter, New Hampshire. I lived with my mother until the first grade. Then I moved with my grandmother for the second grade. Then back to my mother for the third grade. Half of that year I went back to my grandmother and I stayed with her till she died. My mother couldn't take care of me because she was always in the barrooms. I know my father, but I never see him. I never lived with him. At least after third grade I wasn't tossed around anymore. My grandmother gave me a happy life. She was always there for me. I was happy then, and after she died I wasn't.

I was all alone at seventeen. I got myself screwed up with a guy. I went with him a long time before I let him touch me. I was young, immature. I grew up fast, awful fast. Then Bill married me. He was a drinker. I shouldn't have gone that way. I knew what alcoholism can do. I am not an alcoholic. My grandfather was. My mother was.

My mother came back into my life when I was twenty-one. She stopped drinking a long time ago. I don't know how you feel about your mother, but I can't get close to my mother. I love her, but I can't get close to her. My mother is not a bad person. She is a good person. I should feel differently about her, but I can't help it. Maybe it's because she wasn't in my life when I was growing up when I needed her the most.

As far as my father, when I see him on the street, I say, "Hi Dad." He says, "Hi." That's it.

I don't talk to my mother about all that. I don't want to hurt her feelings. My mother is a very sensitive person. Very sensitive. Maybe it wasn't her fault. I can't blame her for anything because I don't know. We never really talked about it. Oh, she's told me some things about my father—how my grandmother bought me a crib and my father sold it before I ever slept in it. Things like that.

I married my husband because I needed somebody. We were married when I was twenty-two. We just went

through life for ten years, then he got hit with being sick, and everything changed. Everything changed. I had a very bad time when my husband got sick. I think that's why the kids—we have four—are acting the way they are now. I should have been there. I mean, I was there, but not there, you know what I mean? I always feel guilty. Probably everything in the whole world is my fault. I feel as if it is. I work as hard as I can, but it's never enough, it's never enough. And I know there are people who have a worse time than I do!

We've been married for twenty-two years. I married my husband for better or worse—that's a value my grandmother taught me. I care for him, don't get me wrong, but I don't think we were made for each other. He's a little guy. I'm a big woman. I always had a guilt complex about that. I love him and he loves me, but we're like night and day. We don't talk, we don't communicate. He holds things bottled up inside him, and I don't. I'm a very emotional person. Well, he went through a hell of a lot; he is living in his own misery. I wouldn't want to be in his place—sick at thirty-three, have to lose a leg. My husband is good to me, don't get me wrong, but there has got to be something more out of a marriage. Do I sound stupid? 'Course, it could be me, too. We lost a lot of things along the way.

I've tried so many things to help him. I forced him to get his license. I got the permit, I filled it out, you know what I mean? He don't go out of the house unless I take him. I have to force him to go to bingo with me. He has a good time, but he gets so nervous, he even gets blotches. He gets hives when he goes near a doctor.

Drinking does not help. Every day I go to the package store and get his beer. My footprints lead right up to the store. People say, "Why do you go? Tell him to get it himself." I can't do that. He can barely stand to do the dishes.

I do an awful lot of crying. I do everything to punish myself. I have asthma, and I smoke cigarettes. I have an ulcer, and I eat everything that is wrong for me. I probably don't go to ALANON because it might make me feel better. I punish myself all the time, and I don't know what I did wrong!

I don't want to be fat, but I can't seem to do anything about it. Does that sound stupid? I tried. My sister-in-law, my girl friend, and me, we joined Women's World. We went seven days a week. I lost sixty-three pounds. That was 1980 I did that; I was thirty-eight years old. I thought it would change my life. It did for a while, but I just got back into the same old grind again. I want to do it again, but I just can't bring myself to. I haven't got any push.

I made my bed and now I am laying in it. I think that's why I read my romances —it's a different world. Working at the shoe shop makes me real tired. I don't do much of anything. I get up and go to work. I come home and I go lay down and I read my books—Harlequins, any romantic novel, historical romances. They're my fantasy since we don't have a sex life or nothing.

My favorite book is *Shanna*. It's an historical romance. You're not going to laugh at me are you? The man and the woman end up falling in love. He loved her, and he was going to do everything in his power to get her. He was rich in his own right. He worked his way up to being a man of means. It's fantasy, it's just fantasy. But that isn't real life.

Did you ever watch "Father Knows Best"? Did you ever believe that families could be like that? But it's not true! He was in charge, totally in charge. It just isn't like that, but you wish it was.

Money is the main thing. My machine in the shop. If it doesn't work right, I get very upset. To the point that I cry. If it's not right, I can't work. You understand all this has to do with money? Because

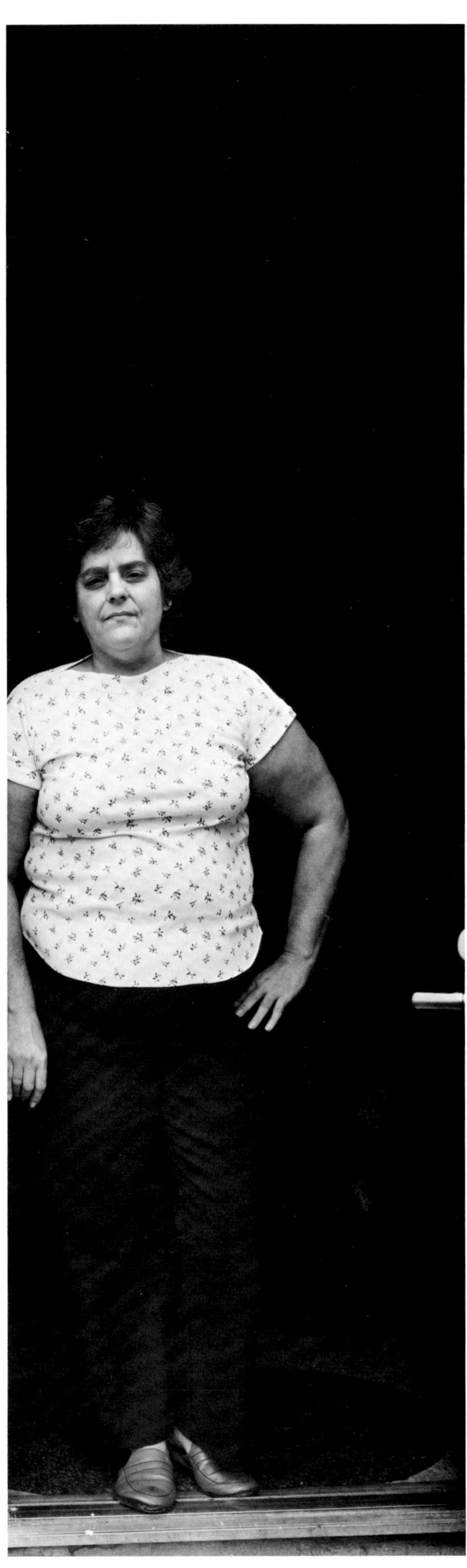

you have to have money to live, and if it ain't working right, then who suffers? I do.

I get mad when I look at other people who have a better life. I'm jealous of people who have money. I work so hard and feel as though I have nothing. I don't know if money is everything, but it has a lot to do with it.

My sister-in-law and me used to be very close. All of a sudden we just stopped. I cut it right off. It was Christmastime, and I couldn't get my kids nothin', and her kids have everything. It's jealousy. It just got away with me. I bought each of the kids a pair of pants and I felt so guilty, but what could I do?

Depression is so awful. I'm just existing, going through the motions. We went to the mental health clinic, and they told us if we straightened ourselves out—my husband and I—that the children would straighten out. We went as a group and singly. They talked to me alone. I don't know if it's me or not.

The man at the clinic told me if I didn't like the situation at home to get out of it. How can you do that? I have three children still at home. A modern woman would just leave in my situation, wouldn't be unhappy all the time. But I won't. Maybe I'm afraid I wouldn't be able to survive by myself, I don't know. But it's me that keeps the family together.

I've tried all the drugs for depression. I've got tranquilizers in my pocketbook right now, but I don't take them. They don't do anything.

I never knew what marijuana was till I was thirty. I started smoking it when Bill was in the hospital having his leg amputated. I smoked it heavy, terribly heavy, for eight, nine years. Daily, nightly, in the morning on the way to work. But you become a fruitcake if you smoke that all the time. I stopped because I didn't like the feeling I was getting anymore.

Smoking so heavy was a very bad thing for me to do because I needed all my

LIFE SUCKS

faculties to be able to listen to the children, which I didn't do at the time, and it's probably what has them all screwed up. They're good kids, don't get me wrong, but they don't give a shit either.

It's hard raising children. Try having three teenagers at once. It's harder than having little babies. I keep saying I'll be glad when they're all grown up and gone. That's awful. But you still help them out. They are still your kids, they're always there.

I'm like night and day at work, isn't that funny? I'm a big mouth, always cracking jokes, maybe because I don't want to go home. At home there are all these problems. There is never any peace. The only time I have to myself is the time I get up in the morning before I go to work. The minute I come back to the house, everything changes. Bickering, back and forth. I don't like to hear fighting, it makes me nervous, it makes my

PFAFF

PFAFF

heart pump. I tell them I'm not gonna come home no more. But I'm not gonna do that.

I still get up in the morning. What do you call it? Commitment? I don't know, that ain't the word. Maybe survival. They all depend on me. I don't depend on anyone. I'm just kind of resigned to the fact that my life is the way it is and that's the way it's gonna be. I can't change anything. I don't know how to change it.

And now I am getting older and I'm thinking I'm gonna die. I have so many things wrong with me. Asthma, anxiety. I think the older you get the more worried you get about dying. I just don't want to have to worry anymore. I'm tired of taking care of everyone; I want someone to take care of me. I'd like an apartment all on one floor. Maybe if everything was on one floor, my husband would come to bed.

I hope someday to be happy.

Celia Alvarez

I was born in Coney Island Hospital and grew up in the projects down by the Brooklyn Navy Yard. Now I am in Queens, where I have lived for six years. I like neighborhoods that are mixed racially and ethnically; it's more reflective of my own life-style. I chose a place that felt comfortable in terms of who I am—a Puerto Rican, single, working-class woman.

I like living by myself. I have lived with other people, but after graduate school I chose to live alone to find out who I was aside from all the things I can be to other people. It's why I haven't gotten involved yet with children of my own and, even to a certain extent, with a long-term relationship.

Within my cultural tradition, I am kind of old not to be married and have kids—not to have played out certain things—so my neighbors, my family, and I, we struggle around it. My mother has the hardest time trying to figure out how I could live alone, why I *want* to be alone. But she is too choosy about who I should be with! You can't win!

It's not like I haven't tried! I have dated a number of different men, and *that* sometimes doesn't make her very happy. I was seeing a Filipino brother, and she said, "Filipino!" When the man I was seeing was African, she said, "African!" My sister married a black American and that was traumatic for my parents, but they got over it. And they'll get over whoever I marry. If I marry. As long as they see the person cares for me and can relate to them. If you speak Spanish, honey, you are in my mother's corner—no matter where you come from. She just doesn't want to feel outside. It's understandable.

Celia talking with neighbors in Jackson Heights

My mother came to the States from Puerto Rico to work in the sewing factories of New York. She married my father, had us three kids one after the other, and didn't work outside the house until we were much older. Her way was to be in the house, with the family, though she regularly took care of the children of other working women in the neighborhood.

My father and his family migrated here, following an aunt of mine—the person I most identify with in my family. She has always led a very independent life. She was able to get a college degree and become a nurse. Now, at sixty-five, after raising a family of five on her own, she lives alone in her own home and continues to do organizing work in the Puerto Rican community.

My parents settled in downtown Brooklyn. My father worked for thirty years in a city hospital, in the mail room. We lived in the Farragut projects for about fourteen years when I was growing up—a predominantly black and Puerto Rican working-class neighborhood, with some Italian and other European immigrant groups. I started out in public school until a teacher told my mother her kids would get a better education at the local Catholic school. Later, I was one of a few kids to desegregate a Catholic high school in Brooklyn.

I did a lot of community work as a young person. It was one way of getting out. My parents were fairly restrictive about what their girls could do or where they could go. We had to scheme ways to get out. One day I told my mother, who was very into having us do our homework, that my homework for gym was to jump rope for an hour, just so I could get out and play.

Two Puerto Rican nuns in the neighborhood helped my mother let go of us to be Fresh Air Fund kids. For several years I went to Utica, New York—to the Douglas family. I really enjoyed it. Learned how to make French toast. French toast! It was culture shock because I was in the country, out in the open, I

FRANKFURTERS
BEEF
HOUSE O
WEENIES
Welcome
PEPSI
HOUSE O
WEENIES

could do things like camp out in the backyard. I was just a kid, and it was an opportunity to see something else. I've always been very curious about what's out there.

I think I had to be that way. I was the eldest child, and that meant a lot. I was the mediator—for my family, for school, for dealing with housing, whatever. I had to keep my ears and eyes open to what was going on because my mother didn't know the language that well. I had to look out not only for myself but for my sister and my brother. In my family I still struggle with thinking that I should be the one to solve everybody's problems. It's my natural mode. It also gives me power and control—I'm sure I am getting something out of it.

My childhood was mixed. I always felt like I was trying to piece a lot of things together, somewhat conflicting things, too. I was going to a school where there was no bilingual education—no one to bridge the gap between home and school. We spoke mostly Spanish at home—mainly as a result of my mother. She has always insisted that we know who we are and where we come from. There are times, when I look back, I wish I could have been more of a kid. That's not to say I disliked my childhood, but I had a lot of responsibility at a very young age.

During adolescence I sort of withdrew from letting my parents know who I really was—partly sheltering them, partly just not knowing how to talk about things. It's hard enough being out there by yourself—trying to make sense of the world—without worrying that your family will abandon you too!

The Catholic church I was raised in instilled a tremendous amount of guilt in me as a woman. But I do believe churches have an important function, particularly in a lot of ethnic, working-class communities, and I respect them as bases for organizing a community. I respect my parents, who still go to church. I got a fairly decent education through the Catholic school system, so there are things I am grateful for. As far as following a Christian ethic, I feel that I live my life out pretty much that way. But I am not a Catholic. I have problems with the theology and issues of patriarchy in the church, from the Pope down. It's anti-woman.

I knew I wanted to go to college. One of the counselors at Espiros in New York—an organization that has historically provided educational support for Latinos—told me about Hampshire College. Though I was a little ambivalent at the time about leaving New York, I was interested in attending a more nontraditional

school. I had had a taste of what it was like to be in an unfamiliar setting—at the high school in Brooklyn, I kind of got slapped up with some racism that I didn't quite expect. I thought, Maybe I should stay home! But I decided to take the risk, and I went. Besides that, it was time for me to leave home. In my culture it was a decent way to do it.

Ironically enough, when I got to Amherst, Massachusetts, it was the first time I had been surrounded by so many Third World scholars. My adviser was the first black woman teacher in my life. It was wonderful because I had people around me who could validate where I came from and at the same time understand where I was going—in terms of pursuing my education, the issues I wanted to deal with, and the struggle that entailed.

Even as a young person I functioned very well in institutions. Sometimes I wondered why was it I was functioning so well. Sometimes I almost didn't want to. The better I was at it, the more I moved away from the things that were most comfortable and familiar.

My politics didn't come top down. I found out about Marx when I got to college. I came to my politics more pragmatically—bottom up. I have more respect for people who try to integrate the two. We all, as people, as women, deal with a lot of things at theoretical levels, and it's a whole 'nother thing integrating them into our lives. I am not denying the need to deal with things at a theoretical level, but I'm not one to be preached at, especially from somebody who doesn't know what the hell he is talking about!

I think it's real important to give solidarity to people struggling for self-determination around the world—to the people of Nicaragua and South Africa, for example. But you also have to look at your solidarity with struggles that are going on here: the high drop-out rate; rising unemployment and homelessness; flare-ups of racial incidents; cutbacks in social spending while the defense budget continues to rise. People act like it's romantic to deal with struggles that are far away. I always say, What are you doing at home? The revolution starts at home, with you. And me. Once I deal with that, I can deal with anything and anyone.

While I was at Hampshire, I discovered an area that interested me—a new field called socio- and ethno-linguistics. I didn't want to do linguistics that was abstract and out of a social context, just correlating something with something else. I wanted to do work that would say something about the issue of culture identity and language use among PRs in the

United States, that would have an impact on language policy here and in Puerto Rico, particularly in the school setting.

I got a full Ford fellowship to attend the graduate school of my choice. I applied to the University of Pennsylvania and Columbia—where one of the secretaries said to me, "Do you know this is one of the top departments in the country?" When I was accepted with a fellowship I wanted to take the application back to her and say, Take it and rotate.

It's a good thing that I have had a lot of experience with people not being supportive or encouraging because now, when I get that kind of response, it just sort of rolls off me. Hampshire was really very good in terms of encouraging me not to take no for an answer—not that I ever really had. I may take the longest road getting someplace, but I get there. Because I take myself there. Sometimes it's very painful, it's very lonely, and it's very hard.

I was very angry my first year at Penn. You get kind of browbeaten at grad school, your self-esteem gets a little bent out of shape. My experiences at Penn hit at a lot of my insecurities as a person. When I got there I realized there was much more to it than I had anticipated, a lot of subfields I didn't know anything about. And there were class differences.

Economics were hard. I have lived on my own basically since I was eighteen. My parents have helped me out here and there, but I pay my own bills. Although I have been in places like Penn and Hampshire, I didn't always have the economic resources to be a full participating member of the club.

I had to sort out whether I wanted to continue in the academic world and what compromises that meant for me as a social person. How I socialize is very different. I mean, I'll eat wine and cheese, entertain myself at academic affairs, discuss my work, but I have other ways of socializing and relating to people. At the university I struggled with my adviser because I always felt he sort of romanticized the life of the underdog—the urban poor of any color. I resented having to go to parties where you're supposed to play out a certain stereotypical role—or if you don't, then you are accused of having bought into the system and denied membership in your own community. I don't have to be a "jungle bunny" to make *you* feel happy about who I am. I am still very much a working-class person—that's how I define myself, where my cultural baggage comes from. I don't have to behave inappropriately in academic settings so that someone can characterize me as acceptable on their terms.

At grad school, even though I did well, got good grades and all that, I felt fragmented, like I had a lot of separate lives. I became involved in an unhealthy

relationship with a black guy who had nothing to do with the university. I enjoyed him because the other parts of me could kind of *be* with him—I could dance, dress, look a certain way. He let me be the other part of me but literally took me for my money. He was a person of big dreams and not enough substance. I loaned him money, trying to be supportive, and he practically dragged me down. But I held on. You have to ask yourself, Why? I think it just reflected how needy I was. The relationship was an extreme version of wanting to stay connected to someone who could deal with another part of my life besides my head. It wasn't good. But you do these things.

When I left Penn in 1980, after getting my master's and taking my prelims, I came back to New York City. I had been away at school about eight years, and I needed to work out some personal things and clean up old business with my folks, about how they relate to me—as a child or an adult. Traditionally, if I had gotten married (and even if it hadn't worked out), and if I had had children, somehow that would have officially moved me into adult status. I didn't go the traditional route, so what was expected of me in terms of myself as a PR woman in my family was very murky territory.

I went into therapy because I felt I couldn't handle the conflicting needs of my life. I'm sure, because I could always handle things, that it looked like my life was a bowl of cherries, but it ain't been a bowl of cherries! I struggle with what things do you let go, what things do you keep.

The immediate problem was getting out of that relationship that wasn't any good. Beyond that, I struggled a lot to become an individual within the context of my family. We need to let each other go, and that's hard for us to do, coming from our tradition.

My family has been real important, helped me to stay connected as a person, kept me grounded. We encourage each other to stretch our own limits but without alienating ourselves from other people or thinking we are better. We don't have pretensions. You go to my mother's house, you are a friend of mine, you sit down, you eat. My parents have three kids, all of whom went to college, but no one is bragging, "You know what my daughter does?" That's not the way we act. I think it's because of our working-class backgrounds, and I am pretty proud of that.

My parents still find some things a little strange—that I like living alone, that I like going places by myself—but it's OK. I know it's hard from their world view. My mom just doesn't roam in the same world. But she gets a kick out of it—she kind of roams in it through us. My sister is a painter, and my father goes to my

LOCKSMITH

sister's art shows. She did a whole show on cows. He had to say, "All right, my daughter is into cows."

When I returned to New York after graduate school, I went to work with the Language Policy Task Force of the Centro de Estudios Puertorriqueños at Hunter College. The Centro was the place where I reconciled my academic self with my commitment to community. I like theoretical work, and I also like feeling I am making a contribution in concrete terms that, I hope, will affect some change. At the Centro, I did not have to justify who I was or struggle to legitimate the necessity of my work.

Later I worked part-time as assistant to the field director at the Ms. Foundation, an organization that funds grass-roots women's groups who are trying to empower themselves. It made me optimistic to see women at community levels, in rural areas, urban areas, white women, black women, Chicanos, Asians, take on local issues and make some changes. It was the first time I had worked in an all-women organization, and it was one of the few places I've worked where I felt a kind of mutual respect.

It was interesting to go to the Board of Directors meetings and see a lot of these upper-middle-class women struggling with some very basic questions—basic to human beings—struggling with their identity, who they are separate from their families, their sexuality, their sense of themselves. Before I met Gloria Steinem I had this perception of her as callous, abrasive, harsh. We all have perceptions of each other that come from stereotypes, fear, not knowing. When I met her I was struck by her vulnerability. She is very human to me now. It opened the window to have direct contact with her, dispelled the stereotype.

For my dissertation I am looking at people's own stories—narratives—as a way of looking at their perceptions of themselves and the conflicts of living in America being PR. I am looking at a phenomenon called code-switching, which is the alternation between English and Spanish, and which happens quite a bit among in-group members. I am trying to work out an hypothesis about the association of Spanish language use with Puerto Rican identity, even in the context of English stories. Stories are a way of looking at issues from the inside, letting people speak for themselves about who they are—rather than creating a broad interpretive sociological interpretation based on who I am.

I try to understand who people are, where they are coming from. I try to accept people's humanness—we are all very fragile—and deal with the things I don't like in a way that people may hear it. I don't think I'm perfect. I'm sure I carry my own shit, too. But I don't like hypocrisy. I find it unacceptable when people are racist. Within my own profession, some people have a very stereotypical notion of what they think of people of color. It's subtle, as it is in most professions. Whatever you do is not quite legitimate, even though they might do the same thing and might not do it as well. I resent having to prove myself every time, resent having to be better than, or work at something a 100 times more than, somebody else. With some people, their life just seems to fit so well.

The places I have been—the schools, the jobs—have taken me out of what would have been the more expected boundaries of my life. In that sense I have moved *out*, but I have moved *with* the people who nurtured me, the community I came out of. I carry those people with me. It's important that I be where I am, even though I am often the only one—the only PR, the only woman, mostly in situations related to my work. But I am there for more than just me. I happen to be the individual involved, but I feel it's important that the people from which I came be present. I take them all with me.

As far as feeling a sense of connectedness, or not wanting to walk away from where I came from, where am I going to walk away to? I have never felt that I had to negate or deny who I was. In some ways, I guess I don't have that luxury. In very basic terms—my name, my color. I very much want to just be me, whether that be me as a PR, me as a woman, a working person, me within the context of my family. I don't want this to sound like I got it all together about where I have been, where I am going, what I am doing. I have my ups and downs, but I'm hopeful. There are a lot of good people out there, doing good things. What else can you do but trust that? And nurture it yourself? I'm learning. I wouldn't have it any other way. It's not that I don't get scared. But I am comfortable with the choices I have made. I kind of like myself now. The choices have had prices, but I get a lot of satisfaction out of this life I lead. It's all right, it's OK.

Belle de Jour

I hate that word, normal. Who created normal? Stupid word. I hate the word abnormal, too. We all have a different definition. It's a very strange thing to want to live like other people think you should live, to do what they think is the right thing for them. I've never cared what other people think. Ever.

I've always loved the story of Ulysses and Circe. How wonderful that this woman was in control and could have all these men at her feet who thought she was magnificent. And when she no longer wanted them she would just—not eliminate them—but keep them on her farm. I thought it would be wonderful to have that kind of setup in life. I do that in a way with my S & M, but with a lot of warmth.

I have two trains of thought—middle-class and kinky (anything that is not considered normal by the outside world). My thinking is middle-class in many ways. I have a husband, two cats, a nice, clean apartment. I go to the theater, I go to the movies, I read. I like S & M and I do it well—that's not middle-class. But I can still be a loving mother, grandmother, wife, animal lover. I like my middle-class part, and I like my kinky part. I would not like to give up either.

From the time I was very young I remember always trying to "run the show." Any show. I really wanted to take over. My mother was very aggressive, too. She was very dominant, and my father was very much in love with her. They had a strange marriage because—in my eyes—she seemed to be rejecting him all the time and he loved it.

I don't remember much of my father; I think he was a tinsmith. He died in 1933.

There were six kids. I am the youngest. I was born in Poland, in a small town, segregated where they kept all the Jews. When I was four we moved to Mexico.

Some of my best memories come from Mexico—even though they hated Jews. There were so many different things and different people. There was an old lady who lived in our building who had lovebirds and all kind of cats and dogs. She had white hair and was chubby and she used to read my cards all the time. I used to dress up the little boys as girls and do theater with them for the Christmas parties—that was wonderful!

My mother told me not to tell anyone we were Jewish. At Christmastime they burned an effigy of a Jewish person in the streets. I used to go to church with my friends all the time and wonder if they ever knew we were Jewish, would they allow us in. It was pretty frightening, but my mother was a blond with blue eyes, so she passed pretty well.

I have no choice about being Jewish. I am not religious. I wouldn't care if I was Jewish, black, Chinese. As long as I am not Polish, but I am!

When we came to the States, we came to a cold-water flat in Newark, New Jersey. It was a bad time. My father had lost his job. My mother had a propensity for business, so in short order she started getting involved in different kinds of business.

I'm sorry to say that my mother ran a grocery store. It just seems like such an asinine business! She always thought food would make money. Her dream was to own her own brownstone, which she eventually did.

When I was about ten or eleven I had about sixteen of my schoolmates working for me. At that time, the kids used to cut

lace to sew on accessories—panties, bras, slips. At the end of the week, each girl would make five or six dollars and I would make a little percentage on each of the girls. I gave the money to my mother because she was saving to buy her house.

I don't ever remember sitting down and talking with my mother about sex. The girls on the block taught me about sex. You have to understand that whatever my mother did or didn't teach me, she couldn't help it. She was married at age thirteen. She was just a child.

I was very close with her. I admired her a lot, she was a very strong person. As much as she was dominant, she was not as outspoken as I am. I'll fight my way if I have to.

I knew that I would not struggle like my mother. I also knew that I didn't want to be poor, ever. In the cold-water flat my father wouldn't let us use too much coal. For dinner we each got a slice of bread with some lemon jelly my father made and a cup of tea. I used to admire people who had big cars and lots of food and good clothing. I said that I would never be a spendthrift but I would never be poor. I had that idea in my head for many many years, and I certainly wouldn't have a grocery store!

When I was a kid, a lot of people said that I would make a good surgeon. I like to take things apart and I have a very steady hand. I thought about being a doctor up until the time I became a hairdresser.

I was determined to go to college—I loved school, always had the highest marks of all the girls who worked for me—but education wasn't really stressed by my parents. What was stressed was getting into a business and making money. That was stressed tremendously, all the time.

I went to NYU for a year and then I went to the New School and City College in the evening. Then I became a cosmetician and beautician.

It was OK, but boring, very boring. I couldn't see why women couldn't wash their own hair, do their own thing. But I was a very good worker. My customers used to say, "I don't know that you are such a good hairstylist, but you can sell us the Brooklyn Bridge." I wanted to change their hair color every single week! I have a propensity for change.

I've been married four times, had a couple of annulments. I like being married. It gives me a sense of security. Now I am married to a man thirty-four years younger than I am, younger than my own child.

I was young, about twenty, when I had my daughter. I had to go to work when she was two months old, after my first husband was killed in the war. I suppose I didn't get that real mother feeling for her.

I am really not a mother type—or I am

Belle with co-worker

not my daughter's conception of a mother type. My daughter's concept is somebody who picks up the phone every day and says, "How are you? What's happening? Oh, your mother-in-law is angry with you?" Ach! I have no patience for dumb stories that mothers talk to their daughters about. I ask her how she is and what's happening and then I say goodbye. I can't get involved in petty little stories. I lack the patience.

I told my daughter to just enjoy everything—to try everything once and make up her own decision about whether it's good or bad for her. But try it! I had no sexual experience until I was married. The first time that a boy tried to kiss me on my breast, I bit him! I told my daughter not to be a virgin when she got married. I'm trying to teach her how to be a real dominant in her life, with her husband, but she does her thing.

I'm just sorry I didn't get into this business at a much earlier stage. At first I did S & M just for fun, for free. I decided that life was a little dull, and one day I put an ad in the paper to play S & M, and it was wonderful, I had a ball. It never occurred to me to go into business until a friend invited me. I thought I was too old. A man I did a session with told me it was much better that I was the age I was. You can't be too old to be a dominant woman, a mistress.

What do I offer people and why? What does Macy's offer people and why do they do it? I do it because I want to make money; I also enjoy it. Hopefully the people I do it for enjoy it, too. I like to give the best service I know how.

S & M should be a very loving experience for two people, enjoyed by both the dominant and the submissive—one person gets what he needs and the other person gives him something that makes her feel good. Even though to people on the outside it looks awful that you may be beating someone, each person gets what they need to make them happy. In S & M you're either a dominant or a submissive. I am a loving dominant.

I just feel very loving when I am in control of somebody. For me, empathy is an important part of S & M. I had no idea

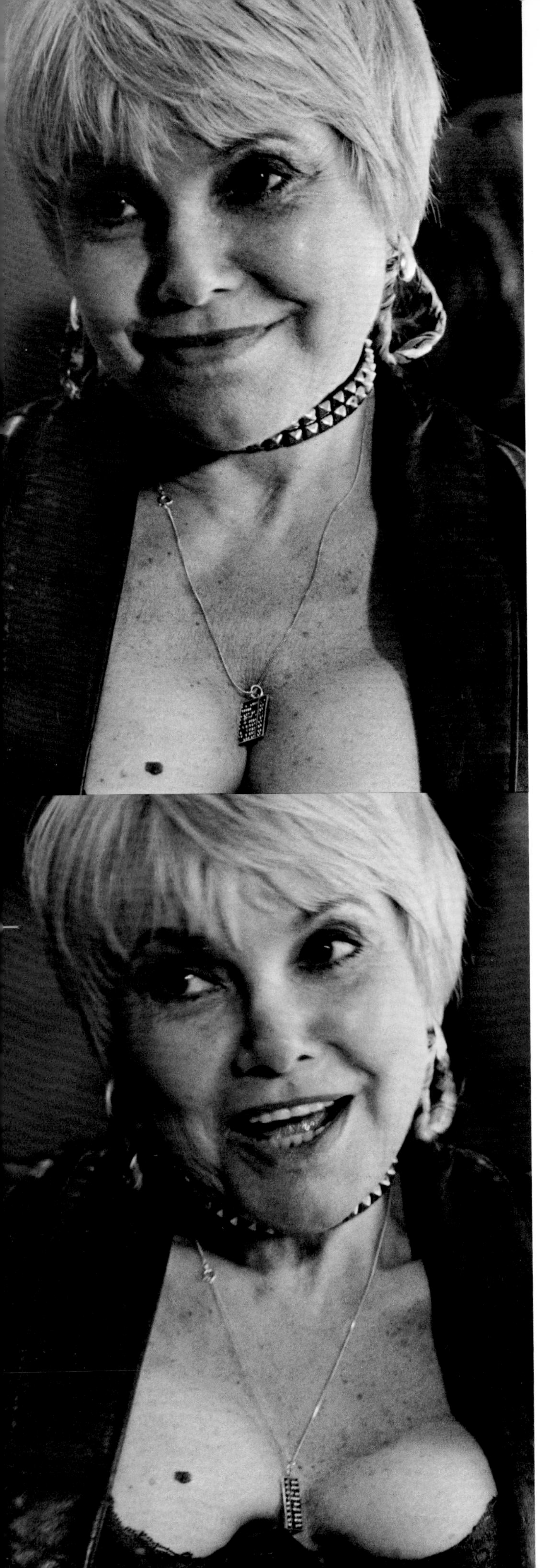

I could be so loving while hitting somebody or be so loving when I stepped on them.

Cruelty is hurting someone who doesn't want to be hurt, forcing somebody to do what you want them to do instead of what they really want to do. Infringing on another person's rights is a form of cruelty. S & M should be about loving, loving the person you are dominating; but whether it is practiced that way I don't know.

I think the people who like S & M have something different in them—something that they are honest about and would like to explore. Mostly it's men who come here, and it's about 75 percent submissive and 25 percent dominant. Most of the clients are business executives. I had some rock stars, a couple of assemblymen, judges, attorneys. Nice people. They are very busy all day and suddenly they come here and they are helpless little boys and our slaves and they can't move because we have them completely tied up. They're tired. They want to relax.

I have discovered that if the relationship with the client becomes too personal, then you can't have a mistress-slave relationship anymore. I don't want to know too much about the client's life because then the S & M relationship disintegrates and you just become friends.

I don't know if the people who come here are happy or not. They are happy when they walk out, mostly. We have an attorney who told us that he used to drink and take drugs. Now, since he has been coming here almost every week he feels like a million, not drinking or taking drugs. Nice, intelligent man, and he likes to be humiliated.

The issue is being out of control and in control. The most important kind of equipment we have is for bondage. We make our slave feel that he is totally our captive. When we put people in bondage we also gag them. They like the feeling of being absolutely helpless.

I've thought about it a lot, but I don't know where bondage came from. Maybe it's something that happened in their childhood, perhaps when their parents punished them and loved them at the same time. I didn't get punished too often, but I think getting spanked can be very exciting.

When I was ten or eleven I saw a man strapping a little girl friend of mine on the behind and the thighs. She was not being punished. I don't know why he was strapping her, but it turned me on terribly. I didn't feel guilty about it or that it was odd—I thought it was interesting.

When clients come here they tell us what their fantasy is and then we choose what equipment we will use. There are so many things to do: I like doing baby sessions; I like doing hospital sessions where I am the nurse; I like doing the mean stepmother session. In S & M I like everything.

One little item we use a lot is a cane; lots of gentlemen have a fantasy of the schoolmistress and the schoolmaster caning them. It's very treacherous, very painful, it can cut the skin. Very popular. Catgut is the most painful thing ever. I got it in Haiti. If a man doesn't get enough pain with all the other stuff we have, this will do the trick. I bought about a dozen.

We have a stock, reminiscent of the witchcraft days. It is wonderful. In the stock you can spank them, give them enemas. For men who want penis torture we hang weights on their testicles. We have our clothing, wigs, shoes, a brassiere with nails inside, shockers for nipples or testicles, little panties with padded behinds.

Some of the people who work for me I train, and some have already had experience. I like getting people who have never done this before because they are more open. A lot of girls do it just to make money. It makes more money than an office job, and it's easier, but I guess some people would rather type than sit

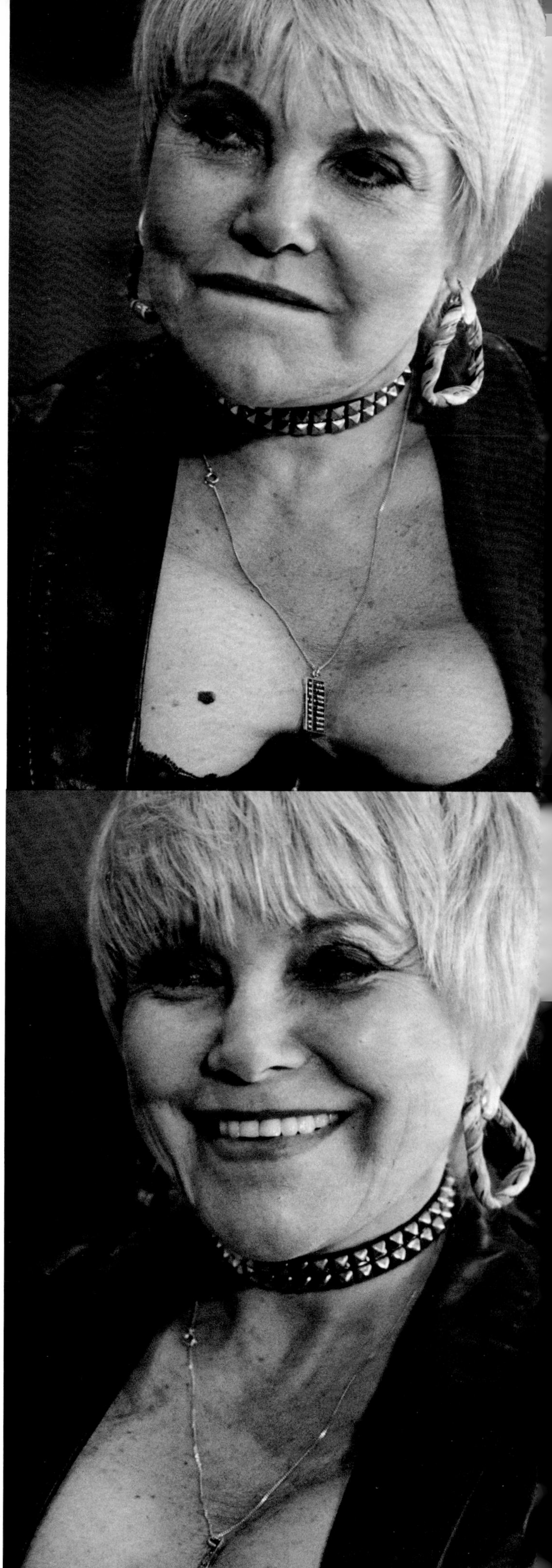

around and wait for somebody to come in.

Part of the training that I give my girls is that the dominant person should know when to stop. I don't know exactly how to explain it, but somehow the submissive communicates when it is no longer pleasurable. I think it happens with body language. I have the impulse to go beyond that point only if I dislike somebody intensely because he is a snob.

People who can't imagine this kind of thing just aren't very open to all aspects of life. The particular message I would like to tell people is not to put down what they don't understand. In my case, S & M, but in any case. I started a theater to show people that S & M is not really so bad, that it's enjoyable for everyone concerned. People should do what makes them happy; and if they can't approve of what I do, that's fine. Nothing is for everybody.

I don't think my philosophy is so different than anybody else's. I have limits for myself, but I certainly have no right to have limits for anybody else. I do my thing and that's good enough.

I definitely think about things being good and bad. I think that anything that's excessively excessive can create problems, but we each have our definition of excessive. I have a very strong religious feeling that AIDS was brought down upon us to cool us down a little bit because we are going overboard on a lot of things. I have a sense that there is something up there, and when you go overboard you get smitten down a little bit. I think we are all a little wary about what's going on. Maybe I am trying to exonerate myself. There are a few things that I am checking myself on. I'm not overboard yet.

I would say I have high values, but of what? I disapprove of drugs. I disapprove of drunkards. I disapprove of anyone who does anything excessively where they hurt themselves or somebody else. I disapprove of people who are cruel to each other. I disapprove of men who batter their wives. I disapprove of anybody who does photography with children. I think we could do with a little less pornography. But I don't think pornography causes violence as much as the stories about the CIA, the G-men, the cowboys and Indians. I disapprove of anybody who is interested in having sex with children or animals. But I think that anything that is done between two consenting people, providing they are old enough to know what they are doing, that's fine.

This business has taught me a lot. My philosophy of life is, basically, each person do what's good for him. Live and let live. Try everything once, if it's not harmful. Be happy and loving. Be wide open and optimistic. Eat plenty of fruits and vegetables.

Maggie Ross

I have called myself a hermit in the past. I don't now because it conjures up too many romantic notions. People will say, "Oh, I met a *real* hermit the other day"—a lunatic running around a monastery who wouldn't talk to anybody! Who is to say what a real hermit or solitary is? These are things known only to God. People think that solitaries sit in their cells and have visions—like watching television. It's not like that at all. It's very ordinary.

My life consists mainly of physical solitude and prayer. My solitary vocation means—in a legal way—being officially under the wing of the church and yet not being attached to a community. In a nonlegal way it is much, much more.

It's a problem to say what I do. I just live my life. I aim at being nonresult-oriented. It's a way of being, and it's a fairly aimless way of being. Obviously there is an aim—but it's not a program you set out for yourself. The solitary life is each human being's willingness to become self-forgetful. It doesn't mean that you forget your basic needs, but you are somehow oriented toward something else.

My life is not a matter of some great self-stripping. The stripping happens, of course, but never the way we think. It comes with being focused in a different way. My confessor has a marvelous phrase: waiting for God is loitering with intent. It's a very active kind of passivity, because it costs your whole being to live with that kind of focus.

I'm not integrated and focused all the time. I can be a perfect bitch, and my confessor rejoices that I have been a great sinner. Sin is part of the package. My

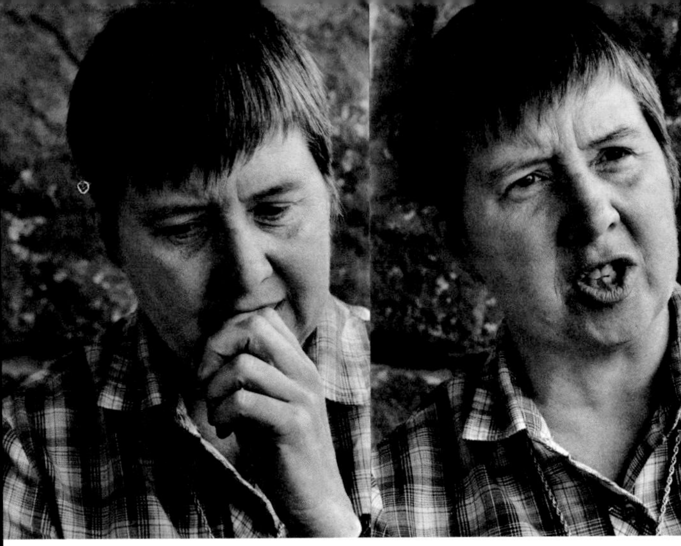

vocation doesn't make me any better or any worse than anyone else. It just happens to be the way I am, the course my life, by grace, has taken. Three questions that I am always asking myself in the back of my mind are: Where do I hurt? What do I really want? How much am I willing to pay for it? If I'm aware of where I hurt, then I am aware of where I am vulnerable and where God can get into me and work through me to bring new life. If I really want to be found in God, then what price am I willing to pay? It has to be everything.

Being a solitary means going to the heart of the world's sin and pain, not necessarily removing oneself from it. The world sees it as a marginal existence and certainly politically—from what's visible, touchable—it is. But quite contrary to being a life of enclosure, which solitude sometimes may be physically, it's a life of exposure. You are not protecting yourself from the things of the world; you are exposing yourself. It 's a very curious phenomenon—and it has been recorded through the ages—that the more solitary you are, the more in touch you are with the world.

A solitary vocation exists in each of us. We know more and more that there is no distinction between secular and religious. I am a solitary the way the other women in this book are solitaries, whether they are doing S & M or whatever. You cannot

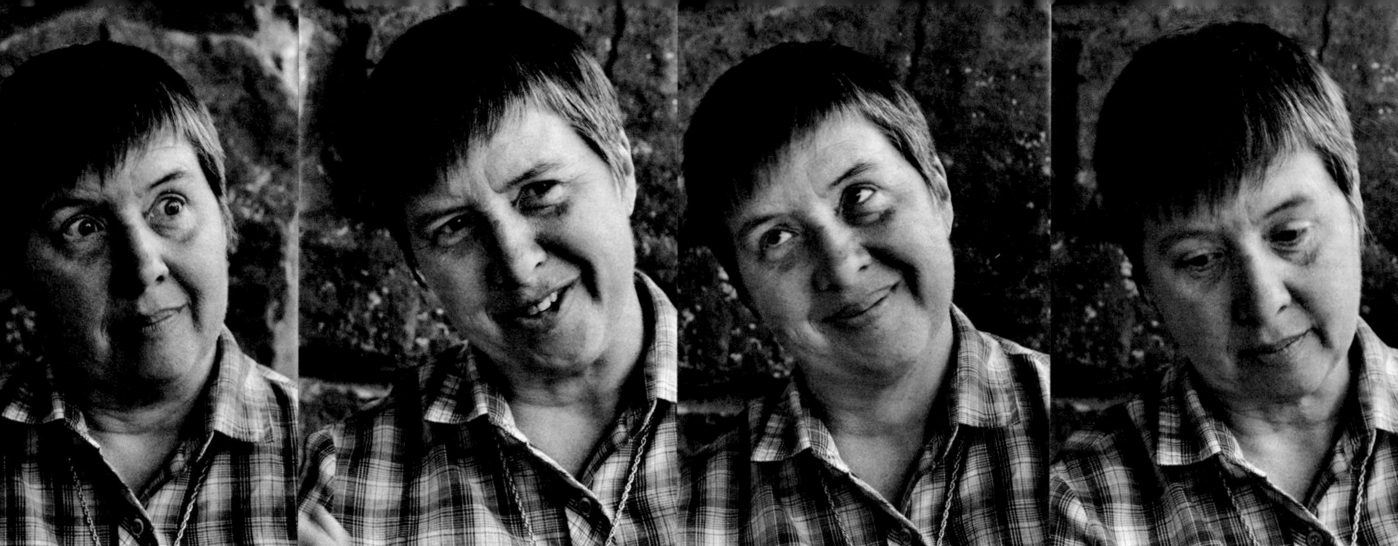

separate the holy from the so-called secular; the two interpenetrate. I am overjoyed not to be put in the nun box. I am not different from other women.

One of the things a solitary is saying is that everybody is a solitary and don't be afraid of your solitude, explore it. The salvation of the world does not come in frantic togetherness. Everyone is afraid of solitude because in solitude you meet death. You meet your own illusions, the sham you are, the con artist you are, what you are trying to sell the world. How much energy you expend trying to keep that inflation going! On a larger scale, it's the story of the world: we are at the nuclear brink because everybody has got to keep the illusion going, and to do so requires a closed system that spirals tighter and tighter and shuts out possibility. Take something as simple as naming a nuclear missile "Peacekeeper." It's a kind of denial mechanism, like people saying nuclear power plants are perfectly safe. Abraham Lincoln said, "Sayin' a sheep has five legs don't make it so."

I don't want to contribute to illusion; I want to contribute to people's sense of reality. I am always testing for the reality beyond bias. The whole point of my vocation is to create possibility, to help God create possibility, to help other people be sprung from their closed systems, to show that the self-emptied life is a source of joy.

Most of the time, I confess, it can feel very useless. You often wonder, Why am I doing this? What good is it? Leading a solitary life, you can get very tired and you can't pray—at least what most people think is prayer. There is often no sense of God in the way people normally think of God, no images that are useful. Religion becomes unbearable, and then there is nothing, in part because you are no longer very self-reflective—the nonexperience of nonexperience.

Anyone whose life is meditative encounters really frightening images coming up. Evil is subtle; it gets in the cracks. You come to know evil better—in every form—as a solitary. The kind of evil I am talking about is not verifiable, anymore than holiness is verifiable. But there is a reality to living out, living through what seems to be total despair, total emptiness, total meaninglessness. But you fall through despair into the hand of God. I'm willing to stake my life on that. Whoever God is keeps me there and sustains me. Faith is the security that enables me to live in insecurity.

My life may be symbolic for some people. For me, it's my vocation and I can't do anything else. My parents have, over the years, come to some kind of peace about what I am doing and who I am and the fact that I will just never buy the family package. Or sell it. They see now that I am not rejecting them or their values but

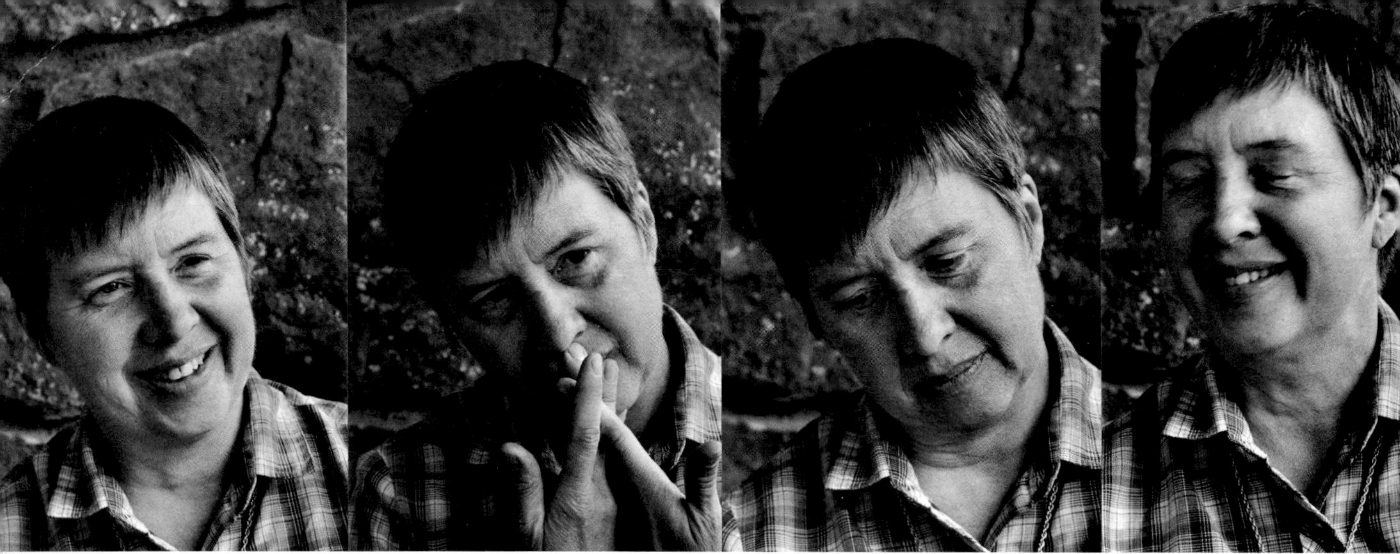

that I have a sense of being called to something else.

I was born in Kansas City, Missouri, in 1941. Basically I grew up in Washington, D.C., where my father was an attorney and in Congress for one term. I led a pretty sheltered life in terms of the average American girl. My all-girl high school class was photographed for the cover of *Time* magazine, with one of us in front as the ultimate preppie. We weren't entirely without revolt, though, because later one of my classmates blew herself up making bombs. I went into a convent—which was probably my version of the same thing!

I entered the convent right after I graduated from Stanford, where I had studied the history of ideas and theology. I think I really wanted to belong. I wasn't aware enough of myself then to realize that I had probably been too damaged in my relationship with my older sister—as children it was intense and negative—to ever live closely with women or anybody else. I finished my training right up to vows, because I needed as much time in community as I could stand and they could stand, but I also knew that I was going to leave: the struggle I was heading for was not something that could be done in any community.

I knew I was much too young to go into solitude, and I knew I had a lot of growing up to do. I left the convent and got into an interdisciplinary, postdoctorate group of practicing analysts, doctors, and some priests. I supported myself by working in publishing, doing some writing, singing professionally. I lived alone in New York City. By the early seventies I was ready for solitude but in despair about finding a way to do it in the church.

On a tour for a conservation foundation I had started, I met a doctor from California who subsequently invited me to come out and live in sin with him on his ranch. By then I had pretty much despaired and tried to kill what vocation was left. I went into a state of spiritual amnesia. I moved to the ranch, became the manager, and about a year later we decided to start a winery. I pushed blindly through a lot of the situation so I could establish a life and not think about my vocation.

Because of pressure from the conservative, mostly Italian wine community and from my family, we decided to get married. My parents were thrilled when I got married—now everything was going to be all right. I remember walking out into the vineyard before the wedding, and this little voice inside me said, What about the vows you made?—because I had been aware of my vocation early and as a child had vowed myself to God. And I shook my fist at heaven and said, "You figure it out!" A very dangerous thing to do!

My marriage was a horrible experience I give great thanks for. Nothing is wasted. It was in the vineyard that I found true solitude. The marriage was great and the marriage was horrible. I particularly learned to love my husband just because the situation was so horrible. But in the end I realized I had to leave.

I was bound and determined finally to live in solitude. But I knew I could not do it in the so-called traditional way, which I felt was artificial. I came in contact with the Trappists, who sort of became my spiritual parents—both the nuns and the monks. On their recommendation I was professed an Anglican solitary in New York in 1980, sponsored by both Roman Catholics and Anglicans. I made four vows: solitude, simplicity, purity of heart (which is what real chastity is), and abandonment (which is a vow of obedience to God). In the end all the vows are one vow which I would sum up as willingness for whatever.

In the first years of working out my solitary vocation, I lived under the wing of various communities. I was very tough with myself, refusing anything not strictly monastic as I then understood that word. For me—not necessarily for anyone else—that was certainly the way to begin. Then on the advice of Trappist monk Dom Flavian Burns, I began to go it alone and went into a wilderness solitude. Right now I live in a city near a cathedral where I worship with others each morning. But I'm always doing my solitary thing, wilderness or city, whatever else I'm doing.

I try to create an environment where I can have as much physical solitude as possible; then I forget about it and just accept the solitude that I am given and the people I run into or who seek me out. There has to be a humility to know when you need to see people. And also the discernment to know when you should endure alone. Again, it's a life of experiment and exposure. I think the longest I've gone without seeing anybody is a month. These things enter by trial and error.

Everyone who goes into physical solitude establishes their own rhythm. You think you go into solitude and it's all fixed up for you—rubbish! No one endows hermits anymore, and if you don't belong to a well-off community—which is itself a problem—it's a big struggle. Solitude is like marriage—you think it's going to be roses with a few thorns, but there is a reality that the roses have to go in the end. And out of the desolation something entirely new and unexpected comes. You can only establish your solitude by going into it naked and playing around with it. You listen for what comes and you do what comes. You have to be very self-observant and very self-confrontive. And there is an awful lot of common sense involved. If you are living in a wilderness situation, there are obvious demands for survival. When I lived in an isolated canyon, I cut and split fourteen cords of wood each year to keep warm.

It becomes more and more simple. You begin to know that just the fact that you're alive is prayer. How wrong it is that we make prayer something special and different than living our ordinary lives on the deepest possible levels.

Now that certain things have become evident in my life, I really don't worry about details so much anymore. I have no scruples about sharing a glass of wine when it's appropriate, but I don't drink alone and I don't drink in excess. I'll go to a party if there's a good reason, though that doesn't happen often. As far as food goes, I eat very simply—mostly eggs, salad, cheese, a little bit of fish, rarely meat. On Wednesday and Friday I usually fast—not because fasting is a kind of magic but because it is a kind of discipline that makes me aware and helps me love. There's an old saying in the monastery, "It's fine to fast but if you bite your sister you'd better not."

Once when I was living in the woods, a lovely lady came to visit me on a Friday during Lent. She brought a hamper filled with fruit in brandy and potted pheasant and all these marvelous delicacies. What would have been less appropriate than to say no? To impose my fast on her when she wanted to celebrate our life in God! Rules are made to be broken—it's one of my favorite sayings and I live by it. I'm inclined to break rules just to keep a crack in the door. A friend of mine says that he stays in the church as a threat. There is an element of that in me. Nuns often ask me—since I am obviously both within and outside the tradition they have—how I discern what to change. My response is, Am I keeping this monastic practice only because I am afraid of something or what people think? If I am, drop it. As long as you are living out of fear, it's a trap.

I prefer a simple life, and follow the same schedule pretty much wherever I am. I get up between 2 and 4 in the morning, depending on the season and my health, and pray until dawn—still-prayer or sometimes simply holding people in my heart before God, particular people as well as people who just turn up in the prayer. I usually begin with the Night Office. The dark hours are a pregnant time. At 7:15 I go to matins and the Eucharist.

I usually do my intellectual work, my writing, in the morning. I call myself a speculative theologian because no

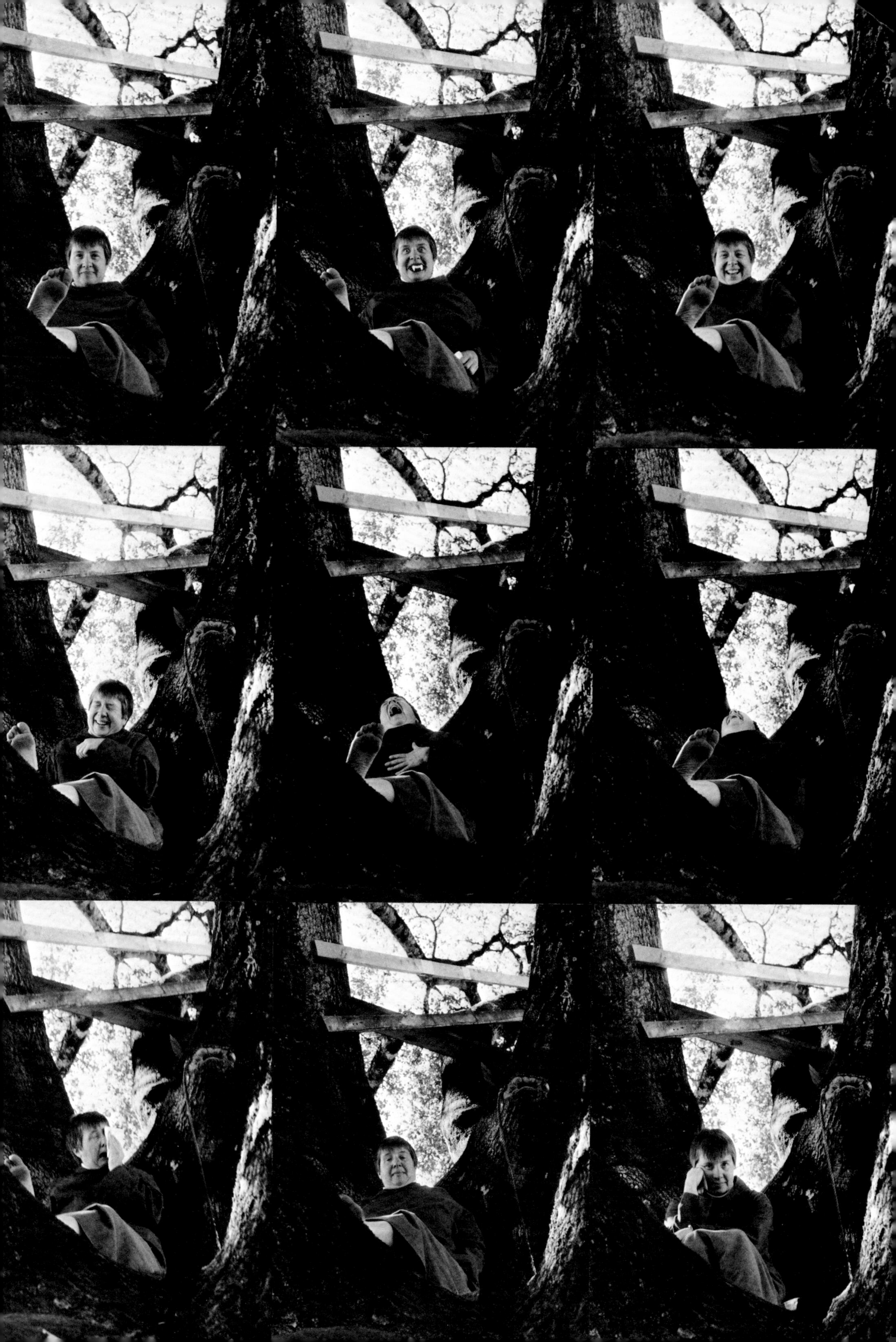

category fits. I don't regard myself as a writer. I have to write to keep my sanity as most writers do, but I've never been able somehow to acquire the persona. I write under a pen name. Who knows who is the writer? What is this great mystery of creativity that comes through people with warts and bad tempers and sore feet and bad breath? It is God's love in the world of the ordinary. In my case, I am absolutely positive that God is the writer, that my part of the creativity is receiving and processing the material through my own wounds. Creation of something new takes place when we are willing to enter and receive what is waiting there for us and will slip into being through us if we give it the slightest chance. If I say anything worthwhile, I want people to look at God and not me, because God is the source.

In the afternoon I get some exercise or I weave. There is usually another prayer time that doesn't take any particular form, just an hour or more of being still. I might say an Office or go to evensong. In the evenings—before I go to bed at 8 or 9—I just wander with God, a kind of availability. I don't ignore other kinds of prayer. I go to the Liturgy now because it's appropriate to the situation. In the wilderness, of course, I'd go for long periods without because it simply wasn't available. Sometimes the Liturgy is wonderful and sometimes it's awful. The life of prayer has its rhythms and its seasons like anything else.

Sometimes worship just becomes a way of making ourselves feel good—good, little kids patting ourselves on the back because we went to church and worshipped the god we projected on God. So much of Christianity today is just a cultural clique. Beauty and ritual are important because they express an inner process. What tends to happen, though, is we hide behind the symbols and almost make a fetish out of Liturgy and the clothes we wear and the motions we go through. It becomes sort of an effete cult of self-glorification, an opportunity to dress up, and God is somehow lost in the process.

The garments some nuns—including me, sometimes—still wear send a mixed message these days. They speak of commitment, which God knows we need, but they also send a message of privileged access to God, which is entirely wrong. They can be a good reminder to yourself of what you are about. If you never take them off, though, you can begin to lose touch with the commonplace. Wearing them can also be a really good way to block communication.

If I am wearing my habit, especially the veil, the great separator, people—even people I know and work with—talk to me completely differently than when I wear regular clothes. I know it's mostly unconscious. Some people just write you off, as though you've had a frontal lobotomy. Others want to lay a mystique trip on you: "You pray for me because I'm no good" or "You're doing it so I don't have to." The danger comes if you start accepting this role of specialness people want to assign you, which is rubbish. You can use the habit to have some pretty interesting fantasies about yourself!

People often come to you thinking that you are some kind of perfect being. We approach all kinds of people like that—rock stars, doctors, for instance. It's the same in religion, only worse. I can't solve anybody's problems for them. I can only be open, be compassionate, and listen. The self-awareness one has to have (in a very detached way) is to know where one's own counterfeits begin. There is always the mixed motive; none of our motives is pure. If you ever feel you have a right to wear the habit, then you shouldn't because it is the garment of humility.

I don't want to be a guru. I also don't want to make a mystique out of trying not to have one. It gets very subtle and the farther you go the more subtle it gets.

Every time you try and make yourself or someone else special in the sense of idolatry or mystique or hero worship, you contribute to unreality, to illusion. Mystique is so terrible and mystery is so wonderful.

I am obviously a sexual being and I have never tried to deny that. I'm good in bed. I enjoyed it. I have been celibate for ten years, ever since I left my husband, and I was sexually active before, but not very. I learned very early on that I would rather spend an evening with a good book than a bad man. And that there is no such thing as a casual sexual encounter.

I see the spiritual and sexual as absolutely connected. But why do we have to make such a fuss about it? People say to me, "What happens when you get horny?" I say, "Well, I thank God everything is still in good working order. I don't do anything particular about it. Usually I just sweat it out. But that's OK."

Virginity has become technical for us like everything else, degenerated into an idea of genital intactness. What could be more stupid or degrading? That chastity and celibacy have been confused in the church is totally wrong. I'd rather have a tired tart than a smug virgin if I were deciding who should come into a monastery. Celibacy is not screwing around; chastity is something else again—single-heartedness. It takes a lifetime to become virgin. You can have a chaste or virginal sexual relationship; you can also have an unchaste celibacy.

If you think about what you are doing when you are making love with someone in a committed and nonexploitive way, you are doing what God does—going to the heart of your own and the other person's pain and saying I love you, creating new life with them. Sometimes that new life is expressed as a child. You are embracing both yourself and the other person, warts and all. True sexuality is a mutual exchange of self-emptying love. It's also fun and pleasurable. For centuries Christianity has been embarrassed about the human body. I wish we could be less shy about seeing God in the most fundamental parts of ourselves. Sex: Why do we wreck something that is so beautiful?

At forty-six I still have so much sexual energy in me that sometimes I can't be as quiet as I'd like. I have to wait for the whole system to die down a bit before I can be as still as I am called to be. At the same time, I know this energy is given for a particular reason. I know that I am coming into my most creative time. My sexuality—while very much alive—is sublimated in a fairly healthy way, and much of it is expressed when I write. It's a very incarnate way of writing—it's intimacy.

I don't engage in sexual relationships not because I don't like them but because they are a distraction. I am the type of person who can only think about one thing at a time. If I am active sexually I'm too preoccupied to do theology. But I'm glad I've had the gift of true sexual expression because it has made me—and I speak only for myself about these things—more broken and so more whole, and it has made me understand, in a way I couldn't have otherwise, things about how God works in and through people.

For some, committed sexual relationships are the way to God and holiness. For others, various kinds of monasticism are the way. Convents and monasteries mirror society at large—I don't see any more or less sexual health in them, although certain kinds of women's monasteries can be very destructive if they are repressive. In a small community any problem is magnified. But you have to remember that spiritual health—growth in holiness—can come to *anyone*, and what the world thinks of as mental health is not a prerequisite.

In women's communities I've found a very high percentage of women who have been raped by their fathers. Nuns are just now beginning to be able to talk about it.

Fortunately we have ways of being helpful. But we have to make sure the monastery doesn't repeat the experience.

We have to see this shocking fact in a larger context: all women have been raped by their fathers, even if they were good fathers, because that's the kind of society and culture we live in. Certainly we have been raped by the church—in a psychological and spiritual sense. People don't want to call nonphysical control rape, but that's what it is.

Abortion is an issue of control on many levels—a woman controlling her own body, a woman controlling the fetus, a woman knowing her personal limits, and men or other women trying to control a woman, which is blatantly wrong. What we end up doing should be done with the greatest care and the greatest listening and the greatest weeping and not with presumption. Abortion is one of those impossible situations, and you'll never know if you have done right. But I don't think it's something you can legislate, either ecclesiastically or from a secular point of view.

I don't call myself a feminist because I can't afford to be identified with any movement or group. I have to be available to everyone. Which doesn't mean that I'm not in favor of the questions and goals of the feminist movement, of which abortion is one. I feel that by not putting any labels on myself that I can communicate in a more acceptable way to a wider variety of people. The Anglican Communion does not take unilateral positions about abortion, or much else, either. Doctrine can't be more than an arrow. Our knowledge of God is unfolding all the time, just as we are.

I'm pretty sure there will come a day when I will go into total reclusion, when

I won't see anyone. I'm too young now. It's not something that can be forced, yet the summons is there. If I insisted that it happen now, that people stay away, that would just be my own power trip. If I leave myself open for co-creation with God, then it will happen if it should. My vocation doesn't allow me to impose my limited perspective on the future. There are no final answers, but a certain commitment to a way—perhaps a commitment to being willing to be uncertain.

Many people find dualism so much easier—easier to say something is good or evil, easier to deal with something that is clear-cut than with something ambiguous that shades into many colors. I know of some priests who will not conduct a funeral for people who have died of AIDS. These clergy say they only deal in certainties. I find that absolutely incredible.

I am heterosexual, but frankly I find all these distinctions artificial. I am interested in person, not orientation. A lot of today's uproar about homosexuality comes from a selective and too-literal reading of the Hebrew Scriptures—the scripture of a culture which deliberately rejected nature and nature worship and therefore knew very little about natural history. Why do we insist on a so-called natural theology that has nothing to do with the way God made the world—a world infinitely more wondrous and mysterious than we can know? How can we go out and wholesale condemn so many of the human race? When we condemn homosexuals, we condemn God for making them that way. And the only thing Jesus condemns is condemnation.

The thing that appalls me is the unnecessary guilt and suffering that society has imposed on people who are made the way God made them. Alleluia and rejoice in people as they are and as they are becoming. Certainly the species needs heterosexual reproduction to survive, but I don't think that's the only reason we are given our jollies. It's destructive to ourselves and everyone else when we say it has got to be this orientation or that one. Moral imperatives lead only to despair. Who are we to say one form is better than the other? Who cares? Self-emptying love transcends all roles.

AIDS doesn't have anything to do with God's judgment of homosexual, heterosexual, bisexual, or purple-spotted ducks. And AIDS certainly is not punishment from God. If we will only listen, God will flood us with healing love and knowledge to help us find a cure. What *is* a certainty is that the God whose nature is to love and suffer with us, who dwells within us, *has* AIDS.

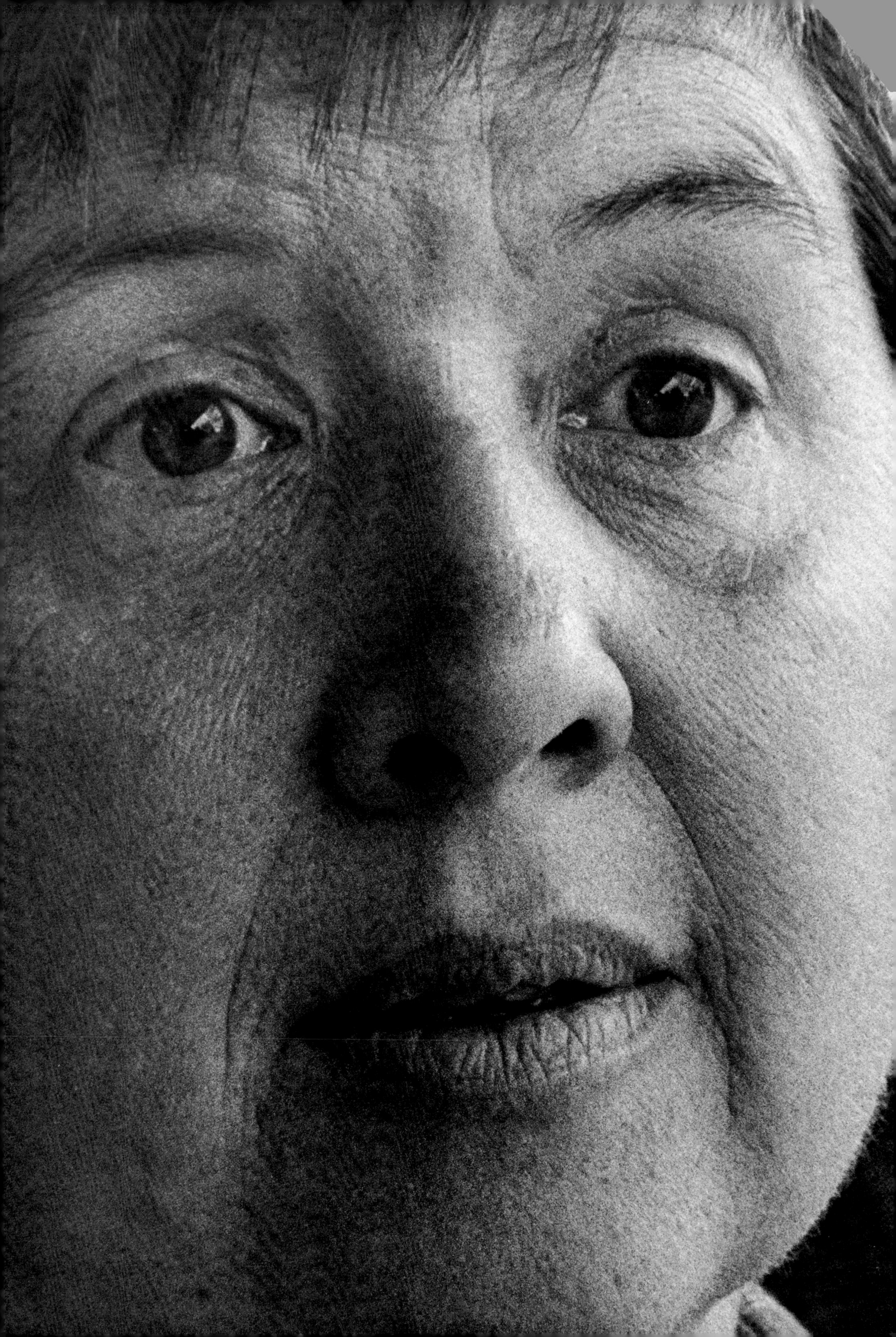